RED LAMP BLACK PIANO

ALSO SEE: WWW.CACAMILIS.ORG

RED LAMP BLACK PIANO

A Cáca Milis Cabaret Anthology

Foreword by Patrick McCabe

Edited by Helena Mulkerns

www.tarapress.net

First Published by
Tara Press, Dublin, New York 2013
First Electronic Edition by Tara Press, 2013
www.tarapress.net

Copyright of individual contributions
with the respective authors, 2013
All rights reserved
The moral right of the authors has been asserted

This book is sold subject to the condition that it shall not, by way of trade or otherwise, be lent, resold, hired out, forwarded, or otherwise circulated without the publisher's prior consent in any form other than that in which it is published and without a similar condition including this condition being
imposed on the subsequent purchaser.
No part of this book may be reproduced in any manner without written permission, except in the case of brief quotations for review purposes.

ISBN 978-0-9545620-4-5

Book and cover design: www.Cyberscribe.ie
Traditional print run: www.Berforts.co.uk

Cover Photographs: Alan Mahon
Arek Wnuk, Filip Naum, Patrick Hogan

Dedication

commemorating

Wexford Arts Centre board member,
historian and artist, Dr Billy Colfer

in memory of

Tommy, Tilly and Tom McKeon

Funding and Proceeds

Funding:
Wexford Arts Centre: www.wexfordartscentre.ie
Wexford Borough Council: www.wexfordboroughcouncil.ie
The Coracle Project: www.coracle.eu.com
Our generous individual Patrons of the Arts
Artists who have donated books and CDs for our raffles
All who have bought raffle tickets at shows
Creative funding comes in the form of the wonderful
poems, stories and reflections contributed by each author,
writer and poet in the collection

Proceeds:
Proceeds will go to The Cáca Milis Cabaret,
its upkeep and promotion of all involved.

10% of book launch proceeds donated to
Marine Watch, saving lives in the Wexford community:
www.marinewatch.ie

  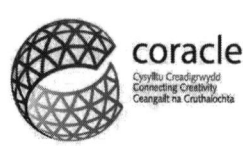

Acknowledgements

(in alpha order)

Alan Corcoran, Alan Mahon, Amanda Bolger, Alex Caulfield, Ami Hiishi, Amy Bolger, Andrew Kenny, Arek Wnuk, Barry Bolger, Barry Delaney, Billy Roche, Bob Cleverly, Bridie Carty, Catherine Bowe, Catherine Gaul, Chrissie Wallace, Cian Murphy, Clare Creely, Cyril Murphy, Dale Burgess, Danny Forde, Declan Cody, Declan Meade, Deirdre Wadding, Denise Scallan, Dermot Bolger, Dominic Taylor, Dominic Willliams, Edwina Forkin, Eleanor McEvoy, Elizabeth Whyte, Emily Whelan, Eoin Colfer, Ewa Neumann, Ferdia MacAnna, Filip Naum, Fintan Cleary, Gerard Hore, Helen Mulkerns, Imogen Robb, Jackie Hayden, Jack L, Jackie Kilgannon, Jim Campbell, Joe Stuart, John McKeon, John Morgan, Josh Johnston, Jonathan Byrne, Kate McKenna, Kevin Weaver, Khelashi Dance, Laura Way, Linda Larkin, Lisa Sills, Lynda Harman, Maria Pepper, Mary Wallace, Matt Crowe, Melanie Meyler, Michelle Morrison, Mick Mulcahy, Naoise Nunn, Niall and Mary Wall, Noelle Campbell-Sharpe, Noel Quaid, Ollie Dempsey, Oonagh Latchford, Oran Ryan, Pat Jackman, Pat McCabe, Patricia Bird, Paul Sills, Paula Nolan, Pauline Martin, Peter Murphy, Regina O'Shea, Robert Kinahan, Robyn Gutteridge, Roisín Dwyer, Sarah Lundberg, Sunniva O'Flynn, The Featherhead Trio, Tony Ennis, Sandra Kiel, Sarah Hendry, Tom Mooney, Tracy Sinnott, Trish and Tony Robinson, Trudy Hayes, Una O'Donohue

Supporters:

The Arts Council of Ireland, Ann's Angles, Annie's Haberdashery, Buí Bolg, Cill Rialaig Artists' Retreat, Listowel Writers' Week, Císten Eile Restaurant, Cloud Nine, D'Lush Café, Elaine Cousins, Filmbase, Fusion Café, Film makers who have contributed their short films, Opera View Restaurant, Phelim Byrne Restaurant, Ranch Texas Restaurant, Riverbank Hotel, Sam McCauley's, Shoe Style International, Spectrum, St. Helen's Resort, Talbot Hotel, Taste Restaurant, The Stinging Fly, The Star Bakery, The Thomas Moore Tavern, Wallaces of Wellingtonbrige, Wexford Arts Centre, Wexford Opera House, Wexford Heritage Park, Wexford Book Centre, The Whitford Hotel, Whites Hotel, Zanzibar Films

Foreword

By Patrick McCabe

There is a lot of talk these days about sex robots, where it's all going to end and all this, what with spiky dystopian buildings stretching high up into the ether and all the rest of it, not to mention us all having conversations in writing with people we neither know or see, as well of course, the immense complexities, moral and otherwise, of all this activity being monitored by ...

Well that is the question for I, for one, do not have the faintest idea. And which brings me neatly to the theme of the enduringly powerful subversive nature of the author and reader interactive relationship and the vivifying magic of people upside-down reciting poems on their heads. Which is not, perhaps, in evidence in the Cáca Milis Cabaret – at least it wasn't on the night that I was there – but, as with all good fiction from Ulysses to Moby Dick – it could be. I mean, with the likes of Cáca Milis, really anything is possible. You could even have a fish walking around the city of Dublin, popping in to meet prostitutes in Nighttown. You could indeed – and have Captain Ahab sipping daiquiris at the bar. Of course you could – if that's what Melville's obsessed anti-hero liked to drink on a night on the town.

I mean, where do you start with uncanny valley robots and programmable robotic vacuum cleaners, saturation 'smart' advertising, Google Glass and Google Earth, or to put it really plainly – the world as Arthur C. Clarke imagined it.

Which again leads us effortlessly to the consideration of Rick Deckard squatting gloomily at the bar counter – trying to figure out just who and who isn't a Replicant, decoding as best he can this retrofitted Dystopian future. Before injecting another load of Blade Runner rocket fuel, like an old Irish republican idealist of the twenties maybe, unburdening himself of a monologue about how his memories are about to be lost, in a world of webcams with simulcrae as humans.

But of course that's not the sort of thing you want to be talking about when you're out for a night of kabarett enjoyment and I had no intention of letting it get me down, as I strolled into Bewley's cafe upstairs, a little bit put out that my old pal Blade Runner hunter-man wasn't there. But who was there was a writer of my acquaintance with whom I soon became engaged in animated conversation, which resulted ultimately in my lamenting the fact that Christopher Isherwood wasn't 'about', for it was he who had first stimulated my adolescent imagination with regard to night-time affairs of this type, with his engaging tales of what Sally Bowles used to get up to before the Nazis broke in and took her monocle.

But not just him, for there was the aforementioned James Joyce too to be considered, or as I preferred to call him Shem The Penman Exotic Ringmaster Of The All-Nude Mutton Stew Revue, who would have enjoyed this anthology no end, I have no doubt. What might he have enjoyed? Well, being a champion of the lamplit vaudeville world of the nineties, where Dan Leno held sway in a miasma of flouncy skirts and cholera-shot fug ('Oo you are a naughty girl!/Indeed you are indeed you are!", I can hear him pipe yet), would he not twirl his cane and quiz: 'What's not to like?' when treated to a rendition of Anthony Jones' 'Birthday Poem?' Or Jackie Hayden's orgiastic feat of sunny southern nomenclature: 'The Wex Factor?'

Perhaps.

But of this there can be no doubt – when Emer Martin sings of Zozimus and 'Beautiful Dublin Town', specky Jemser will be out on the floor.

On the evening I attended – I noticed there are a number of well-established names included here also, Billy Roche in particular, and Dermot Bolger with a typically wise rumination on aging. And who, many years ago, published my own first effort.

Another aspect of my evening at the Cáca Milis Cabaret included discussions with a variety of individuals regarding the nature of art and existence – I don't know what the world is coming to – but I'll tell you this: in a world of fibre optics and GCHQ, I'm with Deckard at the bar.

For I know who the Replicants are. And they won't be found, believe me, Chez Mulkerns. Did you know that her grandfather was The Rajah Of Frongoch? Yes, no better man for putting on shows in prisons, way back then when establishing the Irish Republic. So she didn't lick it off the briars, as they say.

I was wondering, when I went in, was it maybe a kind of competition. Along the lines of that which developed between Patrick Kavanagh and another local scribe, many moons ago. 'How much do you charge per line?', a potential customer once inquired of the Monaghan master. Only to receive the reply: 'Five shillings to you.' Well, not to him as events were to transpire, for Kavanagh never heard from him again. Only to meet him one day in Dundalk. 'You never came back to me about the pome for your daughter's wedding?' 'Naw I didn't,' said he, 'And won't. For there's a man in Essexford and does it for one and six. And he'd poet the shite out of you any day, Kavanagh!'

The night I stepped in, I thought of John Hinde: as if the great photographer of the sixties had turned his lens on night-time in Dublin. But then, as was his wont, ensured that the original transparencies were enhanced, the colour of clothes altered and the dull Irish skies replaced with a brighter post-midnite Mediterranean version. And which is precisely the kind of alchemy this book achieves, filled with nuggets and wonders too numerous, regrettably, for all of them to be named here, whether established or emerging: but they include Kevin Connelly and Margaret Breen, The Walls-Eamonn and Niall, and Oran Ryan and Patrick Chapman, Kate Dempsey and Jim Maguire. Did you know that Eoin Colfer is making a Disney movie? Well, he's here too: with a cracker about a seal.

Beir Bua, red lamp on the black piano. Or, as 'Papa' Hemmingway used to say to Joyce whenever the Fontenoy Street man posed the question, 'do you think that art can ever hope to meet the threat of the astral assassins?'

'It can surely, James – haven't you been down to see Helena's Cáca Milis?'

Patrick Mc Cabe, August 2013.

Table of Contents

Foreword – Patrick McCabe	ix
Preface	iv
The Jump - Paul Tylak	19
Cut – Patrick Chapman	29
Lifeguard - Drucilla Wall	30
The Loan - Susan Lanigan	32
Birthday Poem – Anthony Jones	43
The Gardener	44
I Sing Of Beauteous Dublin Town – Emer Martin	48
Only Us – Jim Maguire	54
The Full Experience – Kate Dempsey	56
Sounds of the River – Peter Murphy	58
While we Sleep – Dermot Bolger	65
Love and Loss – Niall Wall	70
Christmas 1947 Preliminary Design for a Universe Circling Spaceship – Oran Ryan	71
Hamburg Woman's Song – Philip Casey	74
Community Matters – Clare Scott	76
The Seal's Fate – Eoin Colfer	78
Facepainting – Erin Fornoff	93
No rain in the desert – Simone Mansell-Broome	95
The Wex Factor – Jackie Hayden	97
Recycled – Paul Harris	101

Autumn, in a time of Climate Change	
Kevin Connelly	103
The Impossible Lasagna – Dave Lordan	104
Loose Haiku – Maeve O'Sullivan	107
The Day Off – Billy Roche	108
In the centre – Chris Ozzard	123
Watermarks – Suzanne Power	127
Mare Rubrum – Helena Mulkerns	130
Lines Inspired By Flamenco Sketches	
Tom Mooney	138
Asylum – excerpt from *Restless Spirit*,	
Margaret Hawkins	143
You Asked if The Cold Weather Reminded	
Me Of Home – Sarah Maria Griffin	148
Mary's Bar – Dominic Williams	149
Wobble – Paul O'Reilly	150
The Need For Leadership – Ross Hattaway	153
Crepuscular – Patrick Kehoe	160
Danse Macabre – Annie Bell-Davies	161
Finders, Keepers – Margaret Breen	165
A Derelict Site in an Imaginary Town	
Eamonn Wall	166
Revolutionaries – Waylon Gary White Deer	170
Neurotic Girl – Westley Barnes	175
End Notes	177
Author Bios	178
Photographs	194

Preface

Roll up, roll up! Come in to where a red lamp glimmers atop a black piano, lit at the beginning of each show to announce an evening of magic.

A rare enough thing indeed – but more often than not it has graced most nights at The Cáca Milis Cabaret since its kick-off in 2009 in the Wexford Arts Centre. It originates from the artist onstage into the air of the darkened theatre, weaving its way around the audience in a subtle – or sometimes clumsy dance. It filters down from the wizardry of the sound desk, or up as people tap the wooden floor to an irresistible beat, and flickers through the tiny flames of candles on every table.

Music, poetry, original song, spoken word, dance, poetry, short film, mime, comedy, storytelling, improv, the circus arts – the Cabaret's cornucopia has delivered everything from internationally known professionals to the glorious first offerings of emerging talent.

Adapting the time-honoured Vaudevillian format, The Cáca Milis doesn't promise perfection, or even consistency, but seeks instead to showcase craft that is true, to an audience that is keen, and yet with no room for pomposity.

It's there when the mike stand keels over, and when an author discards his best-seller on the piano and launches into a 15-minute comic monologue. There when two musicians who have never met duet a breathtaking, impromptu classic.

Red Lamp Black Piano features a selection of the writers and poets who have participated in The Cáca Milis Cabaret over the last few years. Proceeds will go back, gratefully, into its upkeep and development.

Almost five years ago, when Elizabeth Whyte persuaded me to start up the Cabaret, I said, "there is a magic in something like this, but it only lasts so long ... "

The amazing thing is that the magic has lasted: due every time, of course, to the talent of the artists and performers who join us onstage. It seeps from the walls of the historic venue, which as been a dancehall, a boxing ring and a courthouse! It comes from the supportive audience who come time and again to listen, appreciate and enjoy it (and occasionally moan!).

It's also created by every person who has helped out, taken bookings, prepared a grant application, worked quirky website coding, edited videos, taken great photos, lit the stage, put away the chairs, sold raffle tickets.

My thanks to Elizabeth Whyte and Helen Mulkerns, whose unfailing frienship and support have been invaluable throughout. And special thanks to Alex Caulfield, without whose constant dedication and hard work as Events Manager, the Cabaret would not have survived past 2010. Lastly, a toast – to the long-gone but not forgotten Jimmie Mulkerns, who was the original inspiration for it all.

Deepest thanks to the writers and poets whose work we have the honour to present in this anthology, because it is they who will, in print at last, capture a little of that elusive magic.

Helena Mulkerns, Editor

RED LAMP BLACK PIANO

The Jump
Paul Tylak

Terry Foyle wasn't looking forward to this. Not one of his better ideas, he was beginning to realise. In fact, that was a sweeping understatement. The truth was, of all the dumb things he had packed into his thirty-two years, this latest escapade was, without a doubt, the most fundamentally, unequivocally, downright *stupid* of all.

Oh well... he thought, as clouds flashed by the oval window ... *could have been worse, I could have died slowly, of old age.* Irrational optimism ran in the family, along with OCD, chestiness, and periods of abject poverty.

He'd seen the ad a week ago, while flicking through a 'Lad-Mag,' consisting of a picture of Mandy Minx, the "glamma-stunna" turned TV presenter, in military-style lingerie, pointing her *whacky* gun-shaped microphone at the camera, a blue square full of white text semi-obscuring her silicone-pumped breasts.

"So you think you're tough? Think you're a survivor? Think you've got what it takes to take on everything I've got?" He didn't think any of these things, but was mildly intrigued. "If so, you could be one of the ten lucky, plucky contestants picked for the new series of my latest prime-time smash-hit sensation, TOTAL CHALLENGE."

Doubt it, he thought, slurping up his pot noodle.

"First prize 3 million euro." *Three million?* Now that

did hold a certain indefinable allure, which he quickly set about defining, with the phrase *Goodbye rat-race, hello endless party* springing to mind. He rang the number given. The receptionist told him when to visit the Selection Office for Irish Total Challenge Wannabees, the following afternoon.

Next day, he darted through the cobbled maze of Temple Bar, and joined a huge queue. Gradually, the proposed interview time became a vague, irrelevant memory.

After several hours of shuffling, immersed in the idle banter of teens and twenty-somethings, which made him simultaneously sad and glad to be older, his turn came, and a chirpy, ultra-skinny production assistant, with frizzy multi-coloured hair and a gratuitous scream-giggle, brought him down a long corridor and into a high-ceilinged, white room. Telling him *The Selection Panel* would be along "in a tick", she gestured towards a large black leather armchair in the middle of the floor, facing a row of plastic orange school chairs. He sat down and was engulfed by loose upholstering. Miss Frizzy-Dizzy left in a sudden inexplicable fit of screaming giggularity.

The room was silent except for the groaning creak of the chair, which Terry felt was slowly, subtly gripping, and possibly digesting him. He observed the large classroom clock on the wall. Occasionally, the second hand stopped, and then skipped ahead a few seconds. Its capriciousness gave him a sense of mortality, of the fleeting, impulsive nature of life.

Just as he was about to pick his nose, *The Selection Panel* filed into the room. They smiled broadly, conferred briefly, and sat and perused their notes on him, which consisted of his name and phone number. In the ensuing silence, he wondered if anyone could see the panic growing on his face.

Suddenly, the Panel launched volley upon volley of highly personal and probing questions.

"Why do you want to do Total Challenge?"

"How many friends have you got?"

"Did your parents love you?"

"Do you mind being ugly?"

"Have you ever had intercourse with an animal? A vegetable?"

"Have you ever contemplated suicide?"

After the initial shock, he settled in, fabricating answers to the more inflammatory questions, weaving what he hoped was a convincing tapestry, an amalgam of his true past and a fantasy background, replete with made-up hobbies, and some *most embarrassing moments* that had never actually happened.

Of course, he didn't mention he'd been deemed anti-social, congenitally lazy, and eminently unemployable by a glittering array of employers. Or that he was on probation for possessing hash. He just did his best to seem like a regular, easy-going, bubbly *bloke*.

"Ok, well, we'll be in touch," said the head selector, and they all sat staring at him, until he realised this was his cue to leave.

"Oh yeah, er ... thanks, bye," he said, wittily, removing himself finally from the clutches of the chair.

Oh well ... so much for that," he thought grimly, as he strolled out, blinking, into the caustic glare of July sunlight careening off the concrete as he passed the still-growing queue of Wannabees.

Later that day, as his teeth met through a delectable slice of deep-pan pepperoni pizza, his mobile twittered. It was one of The Selectors.

"Terry!" the voice drawled, "Guess what – someone dropped out ... you get to take the TOTAL CHALLENGE!"

He actually jumped for joy, throwing his can of beer God-knows-where, nudging the layer of rubbish that covered his living room.

And so, here he was, dressed in ill-fitting khaki, gazing like a head-lit rabbit through a bright oval window on an antique warplane, at twenty-thousand feet, hurtling loudly, unstoppably, to his fate. Him and nine other "lucky" contestants, perspiring with the fear they'd so far been denying, the realisation finally dawning, that *this* was *it*.

He could be The Chosen One.

He could be dead within minutes.

He looked around at the others. Nine faces, each unique, but each bearing the exact same expression: terror.

Mandy Minx, her mini-cam crew in tow, was working her way down the line, looking for reactions, asking people how they felt. Did they wish they were somewhere else? What did their families think? She shoved her mike in his face.

"What would *you* do with the money if you won, Terry?" chirped Mandy.

"Um, well, I don't really know, buy a few aircraft carriers, hire an army and invade somewhere ..." he rambled, his mouth and mind disparate.

"Ooh, an invader! Kinky! Right, thanks Terry, and good luck!"

Ms Minx wriggled up to the last contestant, a young,

pink-faced woman with dark green hair and multiple piercings, who looked like she was about to burst, eyes bulging from her fearful beetroot head. Mandy prompted her with the mic and she let out a stream of pure babble, punctuated by gasping. Realising this wasn't going well, Mandy turned away mid-jibber, nodding and smiling, to tell the viewers a bit more about the pilot, Dave.

" ... see him smiling there, in the corner of your screens, isn't he a *hunk*?"

The green-haired woman slumped back against the metal ribcage of the plane, staring lock-jawed at Terry, or through him, he couldn't tell. A string of saliva swung from her multi-ringed lower lip. She seemed dazed, completely unaware of where she was, and to Terry's eyes, disturbingly beatific.

The fifty year-old B-52 shuddered on through the clouds with its cargo of fear. Suddenly, a deep, cheery voice crackled from the intercom.

"Alright *Total Challenge Contestants*, the moment of truth has arrived. It's TIME ... TO ... JUMP! Good luck everybody!"

Van Halen's "Jump" came predictably over the intercom, but was drowned out by the drone of the engines. Terry mused absently that he would have preferred "Jump Around" by House of Pain. Mandy perked up into her main camera.

"Ooh, isn't this exciting? Well, here we go, the first round of Total Challenge, The Jump of Death! As you know, the ten contestants have all got parachutes, nine that work, and one ... that *doesn't!* And the worst thing is, it's all completely *random*, nobody has a clue who's got the

Dreaded Dud. Not even the *hunky* air force boys, because the packs all look and feel *exactly the same!* So, I just want to wish you all the very best of luck on your twenty-thousand foot jump, and say that I think you're all really, really, *really* brave! And whichever one of you doesn't make it, well, you're the bravest of all, and hey, we at Total Challenge, and everyone watching, will always remember you – "

Her spiel was cut short by a very large, burly soldier, who tore open the cargo doors and began getting the contestants in line. The wind screamed into the cabin, tearing at eyes and skin. Until then, it had been a half-heard thing, whining faintly by outside, toying with them, but *this,* this was a cataclysmic bolt of pile-driving fury.

Terry's legs began shaking like freshly landed fish, wet with cold sweat. He suddenly knew how it felt to *quake,* and did his fair share of balking and blanching while he was at it. As the fuselage of the old warplane rattled derisively through his body, clarity – a piercing, awful clarity – set in. He had never done anything with his life, and now he never would. *Oh shut up*, he self-admonished, *you've got a pretty decent chance. There'll be plenty more life to fritter away after this.*

He briefly promised God he'd tidy up his flat if he survived, his manifestation of *The Almighty* for the purposes of this pact being a fat, grumpy cleaning woman.

He watched the others with the detachment of a condemned man observing an execution, as they were hoisted onto a metal ceiling-rail, like corpses in an abattoir, and then, after a brief flurry of thumbs-ups, were literally flung out the door.

That'll be me in a minute, he mused. He was seventh,

just late enough to fake a confident-looking jumping stance, but still about ten years too early for his liking. For some reason, all he could think of was *Time for Tubby-bye-byes ... Time for Tubby-bye-byes ...*

The soldier gave him a good hard shove, a powerful jolt in the spine, but it was nothing compared to the tenderising he received on his entry into the pale blue sky. He grinned involuntarily, a big toothy wind-grin, as his face rippled like a puddle in a hailstorm. Thanking God for goggles, he plummeted.

After a few seconds, when his ears had got used to the roar of a man slicing through the atmosphere, he found he was quite calm, quite exhilarated by the buffeting blast of it all.

My God, I'm a natural! He thought. He felt positively *nonchalant*, and imagined he exhibited, when seen from afar, all the signs of sky-diving nonchalance. A tiny part of him was alarmed that he didn't give a damn about anything at that precise moment, and the rest of him was saying *Relax! You're having a ball. Why be alarmed at not being alarmed, dammit!*

Suddenly, he fell through several layers of cloud, and then back into clear sky, vaguely surprised his mouth hadn't filled with cotton wool. Below him was the terracotta and white mosaic of suburbia, draped across the foothills of the Dublin mountains.

This was the most terrifying, primal, and serene exhilaration he'd ever felt. Here, with the wind nearly ripping his hair out and pinning back his ears, he felt closer to God than any agnostic deserved to.

Far above, he could see the Total Challenge helicopter,

its cameraman panning around, seeking out the elusive *splatmeister*. Forcing his head down, he saw another helicopter below, the press craft, closer to the ground, its myriad lenses glinting skyward. All were scanning for signs of imminent death, knowing that soon enough, one prime give-away would be lack of a parachute.

He noted that the ground didn't seem to be getting any closer, which was fine by him. *Ha, suits me down to the ground!* he mused. Then he remembered what the instructor had said, how it would stay like that for a deceptively long time, then suddenly expand, approaching at exponential speed, with decidedly pancakey consequences, if you were *The Chosen One*.

Terry Foyle laughed out loud, or as loud as he could, in the demonic roar of the wind. He had suddenly realised why everyone had found the instructor's description of *terminal* velocity so funny. *Terminal, yeah, oh ha ha, terminal ...*

And now, as parachutes began opening all around, above, below, left and right, he was starting to realise who *The Chosen One* was. He didn't bother trying to count them, the giant drifting hankies, having decided, if he was going to die, well that was that.

Taking one final look around, he had to admit that yes, all cameras were now, undeniably, and unashamedly, trained on him.

Then one minute, the jumper below him was twirling gracefully towards the press helicopter, and next – *oh, Jesus Fuck!*

He couldn't believe what happened. He or she, went right *through* the blades, and was transformed beneath his unblinking gaze, into a blur of thin slices, spun out in every direction, a translucent pink *catherine wheel*.

Almost immediately, the flesh-clogged blade-shaft seized, and the helicopter, carrying the cream of Irish paparazzi, began its final, sickening, ground-ward lurch.

As Terry flailed down towards it all, the victim's parachute came shooting up past him. Instinctively, he flashed out a hand and grabbed some tangled guy rope, which was attached to a shredded leather harness, containing a large, perfectly-sliced lump of torso. It lodged itself under his armpit with a wet thud, and, not being one to quibble, he hung on, swinging himself around till he had both arms through the ropes.

There was a pink cloud all around him – vaporised blood – and feeling something prickly on the rope, he turned to see tufts of green hair wedged between his taut white knuckles. He recoiled in disgust, and his nose brushed against something wet, caught up in the other rope. It was a rounded lump of mauve-pink flesh with a shiny metal bolt through it.

By the time he realised it was a pierced tongue, lolling around lifelessly, licking him, it was gone, flung to hell by a shuddering explosion, which sent him momentarily and violently upwards. He blacked out briefly, brought round by the nauseating stench of burning flesh and fuel belching up from the carnage below.

So Terry Foyle, the one with the dud 'chute, was, nevertheless floating smoothly to the ground and landing feather-soft in a clump of gorse.

After a brief struggle, he crawled out of the harness, flung the life-saving lump of pierced woman over his shoulder, and trotted down the hill.

People were screaming, streaming towards and away from the blaze-blackened crash-site. Flaming human torches were hatching from the inferno of the downed craft, molten telephoto lenses fused with vulcanised hands. They thrashed around, finally collapsing into the soft embrace of the blanket-wielding paramedics. A clamour of sirens pierced the languid July air as more emergency services closed in.

The devastation washed over him, slowly filling his senses; but he couldn't help it, he was smiling – a dazed, wistful smile.

One down, eight to go, he thought.

Cut

Patrick Chapman

You marry the knife
That fits the incision

You never let close –
The slit in your side.

When it comes,
Blame the hand.
When it comes –

The slit in your side
You never let close,

That fits the incision –
You marry the knife.

Lifeguard
Drucilla Wall

They trod her into the blue concrete.
I saw that.
She tried to push upward,
her arms like streaks of pale fish
at the shallow bottom of the waterslide.
Maybe I saw that,
in the chop of children.

Thirteenth summer, first job,
the world an unforgiving mirror,
new bikini hiking up in the back,
I had refused to wear my glasses.
Hold this safety pole and stand there.
Just watch. Just do that, okay?
And I did. But she was still under,
doing a doggie paddle all wrong.
I felt that, so I jumped in,
pulled her to the surface,
wondered at the weight of her head
rolling on my shoulder.
I did not call for help.
Only ran like some big gawk of a bird,

bouncing the child out the gates
of the supervised area.
I may have shouted at her
above all the fun, above the din
of their horrible little minds,
so easy with their feet and their throats
and their team sports and their sing-alongs.

She coughed and started crying.
Stupidly, I lay her on her side,
slapped her back. Good. That's good.
Coughing is good. I am sure
I carried her to the Nurse's Station.
Someone said, get a towel.
Or maybe we were both wrapped
in one big blanket, side by side
on the edge of the medical bed,
shivering less and less.

Then, nothing happened,
plowed in through the door,
the open windows,
unmeasurable nothing,
even into September.

The Loan

Susan Lanigan

Garvan Freehill took off his gabardine coat and scarf and proceeded to the bar. His drink, a double whiskey-and-soda pre-ordered for the interval, was waiting for him.

The first half had been pleasant enough, nothing extraordinary. Of course, there wouldn't be many more shows like this, not for Garvan. But he, an assistant bank manager, a person of stature, could still walk through the throngs at the bar, perch on the edge of a long couch, and pretend. Pretend that he still belonged, keeping up the spell by addressing the barman with the mellifluous accent he had learned from his mother in Monkstown. His bank balance, more known to him than the birth mole on his thigh, told a different story. Garvan Freehill was broke. The barman he patronised was far better off than he.

Even without his coat, the air felt warm and heavy with people. He wandered about until he found a place to rest his elbow and his drink: a narrow shelf by the wall-length window looking down on the street below. He never minded being alone, drinking alone. He wouldn't have come here with Ronan Whelan, his immediate boss and closest buddy. Ronan liked theatre but he preferred drama to this sort of thing. He was funny, Ronan, cracking jokes about his own astigmatism, calling himself Gladly the Cross-Eyed Bear. It had lightened work when the pressure was on; Ronan was good at that. Garvan thought awhile about Ronan and their friendship; between swallows of warm, briefly-stinging whisky, he raised his head, holding his tumbler in his hand, as if drinking to his memory. This movement made him see people he otherwise wouldn't – then he thought he recognised someone.

He could not tell what made him react, cry out. The pale skin? The erect collar? But even though his mouth framed the words, he did not get to call Sebastian, he did not even get to say the "Se-," before the young man half-turned around and he saw an aquiline nose, presentable, but not belonging to the person whose name he had despairingly called out in the middle of a crowded theatre bar.

There were only two people he made that mistake with: the young man and his own wife, Roisin. He kept seeing her – the woman in the red beret on the DART, the girl with plaits carrying her daughter around her hip. Or maybe he was seeing Roisin as she used to be. He was never sure; his mind was a bit all over the place at the moment.

They'd lived together with their one-year-old daughter, Ailbhe, outside Aughanure Town, where Garvan had just been promoted. The house was on a new estate: Garvan remembered Roisin's eyes lighting up as they walked through the cramped hall, the estate agent pointing out the fitted kitchen, then the fake black marble fireplace, followed by the small asphalt driveway.

"We'll take it," Roisin said.

Garvan tried to manoeuvre her aside, even though she frowned as he tapped on her elbow. "Darling…I?"

"What?"

Now her mouth was changed, hardened; she gathered Ailbhe about her waist, as a barrier between them. A light scent of deodorant and Sudocrem exhaled from her skin; her red, painted lip-corners disappeared into creased laughter lines.

"Darling ... I thought ..." He kept going, absurd as it seemed even to him in that narrow hallway of surrendered dreams. Telling her of what they had talked of once, when they still lay in bed with legs entangled after love: the old house by the lake, sashed windows, walls lined with bookshelves; faded but comfortable armchairs, a lamplit refuge in the driving country rain.

"Garvan," Roisin said, "Can we be realistic, please? This isn't your Mummy buying a house here."

A low blow, but not an unjust one. His mother still lived alone in a big house in Monkstown, believing in romance. She sat by the vast fireplace, a cold wind constantly blasting in off the bay, and talked of the writers she loved before marriage had taken away her youth and freedom. She refused to move out. "Such a little, little man," she had cried when Garvan attempted to persuade her, "just like your father." It was no use. Her husband had left her, everyone did, because she asked too much; nothing he gave would be enough. Roisin told him he was mad even to try. Yet he knew he would keep on giving, precisely because he was the little man she said he was.

The bell chimed. Interval over, Garvan put down his half-finished whisky. He'd drunk enough of the stuff, at sufficient speed, for it to mute his senses a little. The people were more distant, chat and laughter changing from stereo to mono, then back to stereo again. He was not a big drinker, not yet, but was resolved to learn more of that world, its maudlin fierceness, its dull despair. Dull, in his experience, was better than sharp. Speaking of which: time to attend the second half of this acceptable performance. He took his seat, realising to his chagrin that the boy he thought he'd recognised earlier was sitting in front of him.

He was in a different seat when he saw the real Sebastian. Confident then, in the large leather chair behind the desk in the branch customer office. Ronan Whelan was standing behind him, a discreet presence. And Sebastian O'Donoghue was sitting opposite, his mother in tow. She talked a lot, her hands fiddling with excess rings, her voice strident from other campaigns like this one. She wanted nothing but the best for her son, for his talent. Sebastian, she eventually brought herself to hint at, needed a loan of six thousand euro for his course of study.

"He's going to be a ballet dancer," she said, "He's got a lot of promise." But he needed to attend an exclusive school somewhere in Russia, as well as some living expenses while he was finding his feet. The mother's voice was clipped and irritable. Garvan had seen this attitude before: she hated having to explain herself to these bank officials. Sebastian, on the other hand, didn't seem bothered or proud.

"I don't want to show off," he said, "but they've really recommended me for this. I've got it on part scholarship. My teacher says I'd be in a position to pay back the loan within four years."

He was eager. Not outstandingly handsome, but innocence and animation made his face beautiful. The suit he wore for his bank appointment – his mother must have ironed it assiduously the night before! – was dark and proper, the collar peaking up. But his body seemed ill at ease, wrapped in that formal mask of stillness. Garvan knew nothing of dancing, but saw Sebastian's body liberated from its layers, arching freely, shape and sinew and muscle all conspiring in the improbability of balancing on one toe. His art was serious and instinctive. There was nothing ridiculous about Sebastian's desire to dance, or to borrow money to dance.

Ronan Whelan, too, would be the type to appreciate Sebastian. "You know what I like about working for this shower?" he'd said once to Garvan at a work drinks, "is the way they cultivate the arts. I mean, for God's sake, we live in a society that gets so fucking materialistic. You forget about the way we were bards, wandering poets. That was the way things were then. Don't you agree?" He gave Garvan no time to reply before continuing, "Now they're building their motorways everywhere, on the Hill of Tara and God knows where – " He waved his arm, just avoiding Garvan's mineral water. Ronan could get carried away, but still. It was rare for him to meet someone as thoughtful at Ronan, in work or out of it. He liked their conversations.

He looked back at Sebastian O'Donoghue, whose lips were parted in a small O of anticipation. Garvan knew that he would pay it back. He'd been in the business a while now, he had learned the ones who were sure things and the ones who weren't. The ones who were professionals, charming you into lending them a pile of money for their own private practice – he'd refused one of them once. He'd got the loan somewhere else and Garvan had heard on the grapevine that he'd fecked off to Australia without paying a cent. Thank God he'd used his instinct there.

But Sebastian – his eyes, his patient face and impatient hands – Sebastian wasn't one of those. Thank God he'd come here. Thank God he'd found someone who recognised that. There were so few ... Garvan allowed himself a smile. The mother smiled back and Sebastian leaned forward in anticipation. Garvan cleared his throat and happily began, "Well, Se- "

"Your application cannot be accepted." Ronan Whelan, still standing behind Garvan, who up till now hadn't said a word.

"What? What did you say?" Sebastian looked as if Whelan had hit him.

"I said it's impossible. There is no guarantee you'd be in a position to repay us this money, later or ever. We as a branch cannot take this risk. This is rejected."

Sebastian flushed. "I have savings, look, I've saved in this branch – "

His mother interrupted, "Mr Whelan, Mr Freehill, you do realise that Sebastian has a very special vocation? Dancers of any calibre are so rare in Ireland. Several of his instructors have told me he is a very promising pupil. Look, look." She shoved various well-fingered references across the table. Ronan pushed them aside with his broad fingers, nearly knocking them to the floor. Garvan put his hand on his arm.

"Ronan," he said. What was he playing at? He knew full well that he couldn't just reject a loan application. As branch bankers, they were aware that the application had to be sent off to the central loans department where the decision would be made. Ronan Whelan had no authority to do this.

But he continued in the same Dalek tone. No, they would not accept the mother as guarantor. No, there could be no special circumstances. No, no, no. Sebastian O'Donoghue, in all his graceful mastery, was not a sound investment for the Aughanure branch. Mrs O'Donoghue's tone, defiant at first, grew by degrees more supplicatory, until, at the very end, she apologised for taking up Mr Whelan's time – Ronan knew how to beat them down – and shuffled out of the office. Sebastian looked back once, straight at Garvan, in hurt puzzlement, his blue eyes wide. Garvan would never forget that look.

When they were alone in the office, it was Ronan's turn to grab his colleague's arm. Garvan stood there, too shocked and amazed at his anger to move.

"Freehill. Don't you ever question my authority again, in front of a customer."

Thinking about it as he sat in the audience area, fiddling with his programme, Garvan regretted, once again, his weak answer – and to a man who had just called him by his surname.

"Ronan ... the procedure ... "

"Procedure? Garvan, don't come on with that bullshit, he's not getting the loan. It's as simple as that."

"But you can't just decide – Ronan, you can't."

"You don't possibly believe I'd allow him to get that money." Ronan, like Roisin, often turned questions into statements.

"Why not? We've had far less reliable people than him and we've granted them loans. He'd pay, you know that. And what about what we were talking about last night? Supporting the arts? Surely – "

"We're talking about proper art, for Irish people, not – these men – these boys. I mean, Sebastian. Look at his name, for fucksake."

"What's his name got to do with anything?"

Ronan smiled. "Don't be so fucking naïve, Freehill."

And everything slowed down.

He remembered Ronan Whelan releasing his arm, walking away. They did not speak again that day, though the team had eaten lunch together, Ronan joking away, the counter girls shrieking with laughter. They all loved Mr Whelan and his mad sense of humour and the way he got on well with everyone. Nobody mentioned the incident; everything went on as usual. It was as if it had never happened for anyone except Garvan Freehill.

He tried to break through the fog and tell Roisin about it, though she, who used to be such a good listener, seemed more taken up with Ailbhe's interest in her new Lego set. Yet he told her the whole story, as he always did. He couldn't imagine not doing so. They shared everything.

"I don't get it. I thought Ronan and I had the same values, understood the same things."

Roisin looked up. "It's business, Garvan. You shouldn't mix that up with friendship."

"But I never thought he'd be so…"

"What?" There it was again, the same intonation as when they were looking at the house. A flat, dead end of a question. Garvan continued nevertheless.

"Well, denying that fellow the loan, just because, well because he didn't feel comfortable with a man being a ballet dancer. That he acted almost as if, well, as if he…"

Roisin put a protective arm around Ailbhe.

"Do you think he was?"

"Well…yes." Garvan realised as he was answering her that it was true. He had felt it, not for any stereotypical reason, but by instinct. You learned that in the bank, instinct, or so Ronan always told him.

Roisin looked at him. "To be honest with you, that feeling – it's not that uncommon. He was uncomfortable. A lot of people are, with that sort of thing."

"But that's not acceptable!"

"And what about that thing? What men do to each other? Is that acceptable?"

And then everything, still slow, got even slower.

It was Garvan's turn to say "What," his turn to look at the woman he had travelled across Europe with, his turn to remember them lying under the stars as they took long breaths from the same spliff: giggling, heady, high. His turn to remember the woman he had loved, who never gave a damn for what anyone thought.

And now, "what men do to each other". This stranger with his child sat in front of him, her face not yet clean of the disgust that had passed across it.

There was no need to hide the truth any more, no point. Not after that. So he told her, as gently as he could, about how he had stopped after marriage, but had not wanted to. How everyone kept saying that attitudes had changed, then his finding that nothing had changed at all, only on the surface, and the confusion he felt between what people said and what they really meant. How people still said "I've nothing against them, if only they wouldn't keep shoving it in my face all the time." How he knew that he would be spat at in the busiest streets of Dublin if he were honest with them and himself, even in these new, self-aware times. How he stayed silent in the wake of other men's hatred for his kind, sometimes ironically and artfully expressed, sometimes not. How he was used to denying himself – how a door could be closed and never opened and that was that. How he could indulge it a bit by devising fantasies during sex with her in latter days, not letting her see the emptiness in him after love. How all this was so hard to say, even now, even to a stranger who used to be familiar. How it was easier to say nothing.

But then they had refused Sebastian O'Donoghue his loan.

Performance: the lights would illuminate the stage once more. The men would come out, jetés and pliés all, followed by those impossibly thin women. He would watch them that night, knowing Sebastian was not there. He hadn't loved Sebastian inappropriately – all he wanted to do was call out, say sorry. One word he could never hope to say to his wife.

His lawyer had advised him not to mount a defence during the separation. Roisin, he explained, had him by the balls. And never mind what they said now about enlightenment and equal access, no family court would entertain a word of it after what he had confessed to his wife. There was no question of seeing Ailbhe either, given the disgusting detail he had described. He accepted that, and as if in a dream agreed to pay maintenance and most of the mortgage. He could hardly blame Roisin for wanting to punish him. Had he had courage, done it before, it would be one thing, but now? He had been a shit to her; he deserved whatever she could throw at him.

Ronan Whelan's astigmatism had served him well when he fired Garvan Freehill the day after; he never had to look him in the eye once. Garvan had smelled the fear off him, the fear all men like Whelan had of men like Garvan.

The family law judge would be unhappy, that was for sure, when there was no money in the account to withdraw. Roisin would be unhappy too. Garvan wished he'd drunk more of that whiskey. He preferred the strange, floating place where great drama presented itself like bald printed words in his head, detached from the rest of him. Not causing tears in the eyes. Now he sank while others floated. Perhaps someday everything would collapse outside the way he was collapsing within, though he saw little sign of it in the bright, harsh, impatient, Irish world around him.

You are right, Mother, he thought without resentment, feeling his head float away with the music: I am but a little man.

He watched the stage, where a well-known choreography was about to unfold. The dancers began their slow, timed movements, their legs extended, torsos like marionettes. They danced, their feet probably bleeding with pain. But they were beautiful, and made it all look so easy, the audience's debt to them invisible at all times. Just like his.

Birthday Poem

Anthony Jones

It was the highlight of my birthday
When we lit the Chinese lantern
And we wished for something better
And though it wasn't mentioned
We both knew what we wanted
Like more money in our pocket
To feed our hungry children

We held the paper open
And set the wick on fire
With red-headed wooden matches
And it grew to its full volume
And climbed above the houses
And we both knew what we wished for
Though it was never uttered
Like an end to the atrocities
We watched daily on the telly
As we ate our TV dinners.

It grew smaller, climbing higher
As a pinpoint in the distance
And we both looked at each other
And we both knew what we wanted

But we knew we'd dare not say it.

The Gardener
Stephen James Smith

She turned to me and said
Do you think I am happy?

And I heard a question
I didn't want to hear
I knew the answer
I have listened to the cry
But to face it
Made me uneasy
But I felt the bravery
I felt the realness in the moment
So I answered

You see she is a gardener
Who has great plans
But works with what she has got
She loves creation
Sees beauty and wants to share it with you
Understands the cruelty of nature
Yet it fills her with wonder
Have you tried her rhubarb
Fresh from granny's garden?
You should!

Maybe there are prettier roses
But she'd rather be a cooking apple
Or better yet a gooseberry
Her hands are worn
The flesh loosened by age
She held my hand in church today
For the first time in too long
Her eyes are still young
Still life to be lived

This Joe Bangles is not condemned
When there is breath left
Still seeking that happiness
God love her!

"People before profit," she says
A modern day Guevara or Connolly
As a nation lets her down
Working 34 years in a job
Draining away her very essence
For what?
To feed me
Educate me
Clothe me
But not stopping there ...

I remember:
She took me to Mrs Prendergast's near Butlin's
When we couldn't afford
to go to Butlin's
Caravanning in Roundwood with takeaway Chinese

The Isle of Mann
The theatre
Tuesdays swimming with a chicken snack-box after
Cinema in Coolock on Saturday
Where I got most of the popcorn
Jazz after church every Sunday
(as we did today 28 years on)
Taught me to notice the sunset

Her bondage
A sick child and a broken marriage
All this
And I don't know how to speak to her
I always want to hug her
And don't know how
So a veiled kiss laced in courtesy will do
She has been learning how to stop living
Inside her own head

Gets up
Goes out
Half the battle
No panic attacks for a while

Still manic
But calmer now
Still pretending
Still xenophobic
Homophobic
Not meaning to be
Lost marbles down gutters like dreams

The anger is fresher though
Built up over years of false dawns and mistrust
Reduced expectations frustrations
Wants contentment now
Quiet
Yes quiet
Peace
Or
Perhaps
Bird song
In her garden
Where she will grow
Rhubarb, strawberries, apples, pears, spuds
Raspberries and gooseberries
Watch them bloom again
And return to the soil
But not before she has lived a life deserving

My mother told me today
She pretends to be happy
What do you say to that?

Let's watch her flower now I say
And bring her some water

I sing of beauteous Dublin town
Emer Martin

Dad had his Zozimus outfit on when I passed by him on Essex Bridge. He wore a long dark coat with a cape over it and a brown beaver hat; he carried a blackthorn stick that he had tied to his wrist with a strap. I looked the other way. He had a crowd of tourists around him and was booming out in that great voice of his:

"Ye sons and daughters of Erin, Gather round poor Zozimus, yer friend; Listen boys, until yez hear My charming song so dear."

I was sidling around the back of the tourists so he wouldn't see me. Neither my brother Cormac nor I could bear my father as Zozimus, but my sister Etain didn't seem to see any difference. And Etain was Etain. She was kind of beyond embarrassment. She lived in her own Etain bubble. She was a baby dyke, with her nose and eyebrows pierced and her head shaved and always with some broke baby dyke girlfriend. Her brown eyes were always open and happy and staring. Some said that there was a want in her but whatever was wanting shouldn't have been there because as far as Cormac and I could see Etain was perfect, and that was the truth.

"Gather round me boys, will yez Gather round me? And hear what I have to say, Before ould Sally brings me My bread and jug of tay. I live in Faddle Alley, Off Blackpits near the Coombe; With my poor wife called Sally, In a narrow, dirty room."

Off the Coombe, no less, that's what they thought. They took his photo and threw a few coins into his hat. He had a straggly beard and long hair under his hat. He came and went as he pleased in our Northumberland Road gaff. And he never had a wife called Sally, but Cormac reckoned he'd killed my mother just by being with her.

"Gather round me, and stop yer noise, Gather round me till my tale is told; Gather round me, ye girls and ye boys, Till I tell yez stories of the days of old."

Gather round me like fuck. Why would I ever do that? Those tourists were lapping it up, though. I'll give him that, he knew how to play it, to fake being the genuine article. It was a gift. What killed me is that Etain adored him. She would seek him out with her baby dyke posse and they would sit on the bridge and listen to the gobshite. Cormac called Etain and all her little dyke gang The Fish Fingers, and the name stuck. Now everyone called them that. Dad was a lighthouse on a bog, a fucking chocolate teapot. He was tits on a bull, but he had her devotion for some reason. Cormac and I agreed that it was the poor girl's only flaw.

"Gather round me, all ye ladies fair, And ye gentlemen of renown; Listen, listen, and to me repair, Whilst I sing of beauteous Dublin town."

"Fionn, Fionn – wait up, wait up."

Shit, I'd been spotted. Note to self, never cross that bridge again.

Wasn't he shuffling after me in his great coat and walking stick flailing, leaving the tourists to stare at us in bewilderment?

"Fionn, son."

"Fuck off. Don't Son me. Go back to work," I said in a low voice.

"Ah come here, don't be like your brother. That's not you talking, that's just you talking so you can repeat it to your brother later on in Grogans."

God but he knew me. It made me stop.

"Thanks, son." He was breathless and gaunt.

"I don't have any money," I said.

"That's not it at all, at all. I need you just to come with me. Just to be with me."

"What? You must be kidding."

"I'm deadly serious. As a wet blanket wrapped around a burning child."

"Don't talk that way to me."

"You're not your brother. I know that Fionn. Follow me."

And I did, I wasn't going anywhere, I was just wandering around town. We walked all the way up to the Mater Private and in through the doors of the hospital. He made inquiries into a Brother McCann. Said he was his nephew. They told us which floor he was on, and which room, so up we went in the elevators.

"I heard he was dying," Dad told me.

"Who is he?" I asked. The hospital was warm so I didn't mind being here. I was actually curious because Dad hadn't put the touch on me, nor was he drunk or stoned.

We entered a private hospital room and an old man lay in the bed. His breathing was laboured and every breath seemed to take him a long time. Dad stood at the end of the bed and trembled. His whole body shook. A woman entered and stared at Dad in his Zozimus outfit as if he was a vision.

"Who are you? Have you got the right room?"

"Are you his relation?" Dad asked.

"I'm his sister. I don't know you. Are you a friend?"

"I was his pupil at St Josephs," Dad whispered. "I wasn't a friend."

"It's only family here," she said, real frosty like. "You should leave."

Dad didn't budge. He went up to the man in the bed who was sleeping and he just stared at him. I kept in the background; I was always good at that. The background was my territory.

The woman slipped out and returned with a nurse.

"I'm sorry, gentlemen, if you are not relations you have to leave."

Dad was so close to the man in the bed as if he was about to kiss him. But he didn't. He seemed to wake up out of a trance and he walked out of the room leaving me. I swear he forgot I was there.

"We could have him transferred to the hospice, but there isn't much time," the nurse said to his sister. I slipped out and took the elevator downstairs. Dad was sitting in the lobby by the vending machines and he was in a right heap. All hunched over and shivering. I sat on a plastic chair beside him.

"Stay with me, son." He pleaded, his eyes yellow and watery.

And I did. We sat for two hours side by side. Sometimes he got up and paced up and down. When he saw the sister leave the elevator to go outside he went back upstairs and

I followed him. There were people outside his room and a small commotion.

"He's gone to a better place." The nurse recognised us.

"Is hell better than here?" Dad said. Her face dropped.

"Can I see him?"

"No, only family."

We knew we had to leave. For all the Old Man's bluster he was cowed by authority.

It was dark outside. I never asked my dad who Brother McCann was. And he never told me. We walked in silence back over to the Liffey River. As we parted he asked me if I had a tenner on me. I said only for a poem. Cormac would have had my life if he knew I pandered to his Zozimus bullshit but I actually felt sorry for the poor fucker. I knew we had shared something but I didn't know what.

My dad looked at me and sighed.

"Just give me the fucking tenner, Fionn. Don't be a bollix. It doesn't suit you. You're a lovely lad. I don't know how you turned out that way, but ye are. You should get out of this fucking kip. Ireland is finished, it was finished before it started. When the ice melted and the first people came. That's what fucked it up for all of us. This island is uninhabitable. Get away from your big brother's shadow, Fionn. Make your move."

I gave him a tenner and he pocketed it. As we parted ways I actually heard him recite something, whether it was for my benefit or not I'd never know. I was trying to formulate in my head how I'd tell Cormac this story without incriminating myself. Cormac had an absolute hatred for the old man but I didn't feel that tonight.

"Oh Stony, Stony, Don't let the Sack-'em-Ups get me,

Send around the hat and buy me a grave."

And with that, off went my dad over the blind black Liffey, the lamplight catching the inky water ripples, repeating a pattern endlessly, his blackthorn stick still swinging strapped to his wrist.

Only us
Jim Maguire

They were here an hour ago
with a gift for our thoughtful big day
and it wasn't all frightful the blue orange
evening and being able to see them more
wanly in the semidetached light besides
kids on silver scooters not letting us down
or the estate. Bravo for wheelie bins
upright and sober again not to mention
the tranquilizing effect of afternoon
sex. Couldn't have imagined that
this morning between half-past-ten
and eleven. This is a good gloaming
all things considered not Armageddon.
To be fork-lifting cake after all that plate
throwing. Them chipper too and so well behaved
I must say. Words folding themselves
into fragrant heaps -- for the usual while.
But ironing piles are allowed to grow
only so high till someone starts grumbling
(between the goodbyes
and the fumbling for keys)
about the height of my weeds.

Nothing for it then but to stand and wait,
gardening not being my forte,
before joining the chorus-line at the gate --
Smi-ile! Wa-ave!
as they drive off leaving you
beep-beep
with this lunatic on your hands.

The Full Experience
Kate Dempsey

As the lights dim, he ambles by,
fumbles in his pocket,
muscles shape his thin shirt,
spicy aftershave,
hair velvet-shorn,
long lean legs, soft leather belt,
and the grace of Fred Astaire.

In another life,
in an other life
I follow him to the foyer.
We scoop five flavours of Ben and Jerry's
and climb to the projection room.
As the film reels overhead, we sample,
rip off our clothes and make love,
dirty sticky love,
down among the popcorn.

In a life,
in this life
I note him passing,
reach over and squeeze your thigh.
You take my hand,
the music builds, we face the screen.

I prefer the front row for the full experience.

The Sounds of the River – A Lost Anthology
(Folk Devil Records) By Bill Howard.
(From Root & Vine magazine, September 1984)

Peter Murphy

Men have always composed hymns in the name of the river. Old man river. Moon river. Cry me a river. Take me to the river.

Now the good people at the Folk Devil label bring us The Sounds of the River, a lavishly packaged and annotated anthology dating from the early mists of recorded music. Songs that will never be played on FM radio or television. Singers who'll never be profiled in Creem or Rolling Stone. Too strange, too alien: six decades later, these recordings still seem too avant garde for mass consumption.

Not that you need a degree in ethnomusicology to be moved by the sounds contained herein. For a small but devoted cabal (mostly intense-looking fellows in black turtlenecks or raven haired strummers in their grandmother's clothes, fully paid-up members of the Shaker chic austerity society), The Sounds of the River has long held the status of occult artifact or musical reliquary. If there's any justice, this reissued and re-mastered version will instigate a full-blown revival.

The Sounds of the River is not so much a collection of

fossils trapped in amber as a virus frozen in wax cylinders and shellac. Mastering engineer Abbie Atkins has done an extraordinary job of cleaning up the original recordings without compromising their primitive (by hi-fi fetishist standards) integrity, painstakingly scraping the dirt from the tombstones' engravings.

Divested of hiss, what once seemed obtuse and obscure transpires as stranger yet in its clarity. Some listeners may have waxed sentimental about all that frying pan crackle, thinking it a veil that enhanced the innate mystery of the music, allowing us to back-project an imagined otherness onto its surfaces. But the real revelation is that what was once shrouded in shadow, now exposed to the light, is even stranger than at first believed.

Previously misheard or impenetrable snatches of lyrics poke from the fog like Victorian grotesques. Be advised, these revenants are even stranger in the daylight.

The Sounds of the River is an accidental song cycle whose unifying theme is the Rua river that runs through the district of Ballo in south-east Ireland. But although each composition originates from that faraway Celtic wellspring, the singers of these songs hail from several thousand miles west, in the coastal towns and fishing outports of Newfoundland.

Song migrations are an integral part of the folk tradition. As indicated in Ellie Bloomfield's liner notes, there was a long tradition of Elizabethan, Scots, and Irish broadsides, murder ballads, child ballads, and traditional songs making their way across the Atlantic to take root in Maine and Massachusetts before drifting all the way down to the Ozarks and the Appalachians. Old world airs and phrases are transmitted through folkways to find a new home on a foreign tongue.

If displaced and dispossessed pilgrims were driven westward by poverty or starvation or religious persecution, often travelling without so much as a chamber pot, they carried with them no shortage of psychological baggage – fables, myths, race memories, oral histories. Hibernian folk music in particular is populated by rakes and wretches peddling tall tales and supernatural yarns, sob stories and banshee cries and blue note *a capella* ballads that often bear odd resemblance to Eastern European and Asian airs.

But these twelve tunes seem to have stopped at St. John's and Mount Pearl and Port aux Basques, primarily because of fishery routes (many Newfoundland fishing folk still speak snatches of a south-eastern Irish traveller patois called *Yola*). Bubbling within this music is the Rua in its various guises: the river as harbinger of flood, the river as giver and taker of life. Many of the lyrics are prophetic in tone. Several, such as 'The River's Coming into Her Time', warn of imminent flood.

Granted, apocalyptic prophesy is no new thing in roots music, especially the North American variety. The Pilgrim Fathers came to God's country looking for a place to face the end of the world. 17th century England was so overrun with Baptists, Anabaptists, Diggers, Levellers, Socinians, Ranters, Muggletonians, and Quakers that after the restoration of the monarchy, speculation about the Second Coming was made a criminal offence. Such apocalyptics were forced west across the ocean to New England, a hotbed of Plymouth Brethren, Seventh Day Adventists and other cults looking for a continent big enough to accommodate their various end-times predictions. The witch hunter Cotton Mather forecast his day of judgement for 1697, then 1716, then 1736. The Jehovah's Witnesses faced their Great Disappointments in 1874, 1878, 1881, 1910, 1914, 1918, 1941, and 1975 – the end of the world as a recurring event.

The Sounds of the River draws from Genesis rather than Revelation, invoking flood mythology from the days of Noah. It also alludes to deluges, dambursts and drownings from the last three centuries. A spoken word piece entitled 'The River's Come-Hither' casts the Rua as both mother confessor and witchy seductress.

'Know this, O human soul: I am the river and I love you, and I alone will take you in.'

The extraordinary gatefold inner sleeve features a collage of telegrammatic news reports of epidemics, intemperance, enforced redundancies, acts of God, shipwrecks, beached whales, parricides, infanticides, filicides, and suicides – transgressions as old as Cain and Abel, all rendered in copper and russet sepia shots and liver-spotted daguerreotypes.

But perhaps the most extraordinary thing about these songs is that they are foundlings, cut loose from the established folk canon. They do not adhere to the rules of rhyme, meter or melody that characterise most traditional compositions. This is what lends them their uncanny, alien modernism. Despite the old world flavours, the instrumental palette utilises the arcane sounds of autoharp, harmonium, melodeon and parlour piano to utterly new effect.

And these songs' dislocation from their Irish musical roots lends them an extra patina of strangeness. Folk songs proliferate throughout the British Isles in varying strains, numerous sets of lyrics wedded to the same melody, or vice versa. But to date no scholar has discovered brother or sister or even first cousin variations of these twelve ballads. Ellie Bloomfield states that at least eight of the selections were published in broadside form and preserved at the town library in Murn, but flood damage destroyed most of the archive so we cannot compare the indigenous with the second-generation versions presented here.

The details of how these field recordings came to appear on the pre-war American market are thus: Marshall Harding, a history professor and song collector from Nantucket, travelled the southern Newfoundland coast in 1926, capturing for posterity the strange sounds he heard at revels, weddings, funerals, and wakes. His recordings were later acquired by an impresario named Lester Pender, who issued them as a limited run of shellac discs on his own label in 1940. Most copies were damaged or lost when the warehouses in which they were stored were requisitioned for the war effort. The only remaining mint and complete collection belonged to a collector from the Bronx named Carlo Galliero. The Folk Devil label then acquired the lot two years ago at a yard sale, to the delight of those of us who for years had to make do with the murky bootleg recordings doing the rounds.

Mr Pender, still in his 20s, might have been Noah ushering endangered species onto the Ark. He went outside the holy canon of blues, gospel, and mountain hollers and took a chance on these strange coastal songs. Of the twelve songs, only 'In the Month of Neverember' adheres to something like a conventional structure. A slow swaying waltz sung by one Root Cooper, accompanied by a mournful melodeon, it sounds like a morbid sea shanty:

'And in the month of Neverember/When the moon was a sliver/You had nothing to give her/But you still placed your bet/In the month of Neverember/In a town by the river/Neverember, you'll never forget.'

And so on, with variations, the singer's voice cracking as he reaches for the note on the unaccountably unnerving final line – 'Neverember, I remember – And yet.' – uttered like a threat, the unsheathing of a knife.

There are echoes of standard folk tropes in 'The Lovers' Lament', sung by Ruth McCracken, in which a heartbroken man throws himself to the mercy of the Rua, and the lover who spurned him, guilt-stricken, follows. From his body grows a water briar, from hers a water rose, and eventually they entwine like souls in the afterlife.

Elsewhere Jack Huxley's 'They Hasten to the Rushes' is the tale of a fisherman who happens upon a mer-girl so beautiful he keeps her shackled with a bag over her head and charges men a guinea a peek. Huxley sings this bizarre narrative with the straight-faced resolve of a murderer sticking to his story long after all evidence has been stacked against him.

There's plenty more where that came from. A breakneck little melodeon belter called 'The Devil's Elbow' (named after a bend in the Rua) hurtles through its two minutes and fifteen seconds like the torrent it describes. But this writer's favourite, and perhaps the eeriest tune you'll hear all year, comes from the mouth of one Annabel Sweeney, who sets her waifish melodies on a bed of ghostly harmonium chords.

'Draw near, said the river, come closer/Place a kiss upon my face/Be mine, dear valentine/And sleep in my sweet embrace.'

Sweeney's chording sounds ad-hoc and intuitive, full of risk. Her instincts seem attuned or vulnerable to esoteric influences (the image of germs entering through ether suggests itself) and her vocal performance sounds almost pre-pubescent, replete with spooky la-la-la refrains. The song sounds full of visitations and visions and séances and mediums channeling the voices of dead girls who expired in childbirth or of consumption or ennui or plain old murder.

The Sounds of the River functions as a sort of calenture, a collective aural hallucination. Its twelve songs are full of surreal weather forecasts, visions, ghost dances, and warnings from the great beyond. The river, once again, is coming into her time.

While We Sleep

i.e. Roger Bolger Senior
b: 17th May 1918, Wexford
d: 20th April 2011, Dublin

Dermot Bolger

While we sleep they are slipping beyond our reach –
    Our elderly parents, frail aunts, grandfathers –

They are dressing themselves, opening doors in
    the night,
Venturing out in search of the first home they
    possessed;

Padding across motorway intersections in
    slippers in the dark,
Shuffling past shopping centres, hulls of lit-up
    office blocks.

We may be scared but they know where they are
    voyaging
Amid their endless confusion as to whether it is
    night or day,

Amid the terror they feel as they sense their
    brains capsizing,
They are walking back towards the reassurance
    of first memory:

The bedrock which for decades got obscured by pressing concerns,
Preoccupied with the business of surviving the business of life.

But now the clutter of middle years has been hacked away,
Reunited with themselves, unhurriedly, with vision unimpaired,

They are shuffling their way back to the streets of their birth,
Skirting carriageways, concourses, each neon-lit underpass.

They are any age and yet they have grown beyond age,
They have become absences in our lives demanding our care,

Yet at the same time oblivious to us. We confuse them,
Disconnected from the landscape in which they are young.

We see shrunken figures in dressing gowns on Zimmer frames
But they are children sent to do a message, an errand of trust.

How can my father be ninety-two as he walks
 through the Faythe,
Knocking on neighbours' doors, stopping
 cloth-capped strangers,

Sent out to seek the loan of a good book for my
 grandfather to read:
A novel with sufficient heft and depth and
 intelligence to distract

A compositor sick of back proofing racks of
 letterpress newsprint,
Who wants to lose himself in a journey through
 unfamiliar streets?

A quiet man who would be led astray by old age
 into the County Home,
Where he waited for the books he sent his young
 son to seek years before.

Gentle grandfather, Republican typesetter drinker
 on Ram Street,
Your vigil is over at the barred window of that
 Enniscorthy asylum,

Your son is coming with your treasured copy of
 the Observer
That he dutifully collects from the Dublin train
 every Sunday morning,

With a Canon Sheenan novel, with H G Wells
    and Chesterton,
With Charles Dickens, Edgar Allen Poe and
    Patrick McGill,

He got distracted from his errand during decades
    in ship's cabins,
Grieving his wife's death, becoming a connoisseur
    of loneliness.

But now he emerges through the far side of such
    struggles,
He has left his front door open, every light on
    deck aglow,

He shuffles on a busted hip, clutching a vast
    armful of books,
Knowing only that somewhere between Finglas
    and Wexford,

Between the century of his birth and the one
    where he dies
He will encounter his father, equally ancient,
    equally young.

His father will be pleased with the books, the
    errand fulfilled.
So while we fret for him adrift in such dangerous
    depths,

Unable to steer between tides of remembrance
    and despair,
A part of him siphons free from the confused
    husk who phones

Moments after we leave his house to ask why
    nobody ever comes:
The part that walks, beyond our remit, towards
    his dead father.

Even if we could follow them, they would be too
    engrossed to care
For the distraction of strangers like us who are not
    yet even born:

We would be intruding on a father and a son
    strolling back from town
To the Green Street terrace that is the first and last
    home they share.

Love and Loss
Niall Wall

heaney and st kevin knew the truth
that to catch a thing of beauty
it is not the clenched fist
but the open gentle hand
upon which a butterfly might briefly alight
and hold the heart in thrall
that it dare not beat nor make a sound
but gaze, adore and be still.

the silent swish of wings
so precious that even wind dares not to breathe.
on them which are so gentle.
that would caress the open hand
as lightly as a mother's kiss
on the cheek of a sleeping child.
which yet brings the adored away
from the beam of hearts' desire

how cruel is an empty hand
which now weighs of dead oaks
and wonders and is sad
that love can be so swift to come
then part and rush away.
how strange the weightless gossamer wing
can leave behind a wake
of sad and weary desolation.

Christmas 1947 Preliminary Design for a Universe Circling Spaceship
Oran Ryan

Before I quit drinking and this aimless drifting, I landed in the desert, where I met my real father. I said, "Daddy! Daddy!" But he didn't hear me. Not at first.

I met him not by accident, as everything is completely ordered and rational in this world. I met him just outside Area 47, the more unfashionable hangout for illegal aliens playing Chess and Go and discussing how much they miss partying with Elvis and all the flaws in Heidegger and playing with Jerry Lee Lewis and music that really rocks on the old busted Wurlitzer in this dusty desert hangout bar. Those days are gone.

There are aliens now outside Area 51, spending their days languidly spinning the wheels of their great minds. Area 51, where the other better adjusted visitors who suck up to the Government agents and the Generals and display their great intellects and let scientists experiment on them and get contracts from the military to build better killing tools to protect and serve. But here at Area 47 we live peacefully with the Christmas Aliens and we read the books they read and miss Elvis and Jerry Lee and we drink and they, the aliens, who don't say much, spend valuable drinking time on this great laughing academy we call Earth.

Dad, at last recognising me in the hot dusty desert crowd, walked away from that Alpha Centurial Beauty he had been languidly kissing by the bar, and he came over and he took my hand and leaned close to me, his face all Merle Haggard, and his eyes burning with that heartbreaking Johnny Cash sincerity. He said, "Son, dear Son, we haven't much time left before it all goes up you know, it's Christmas, and we are stuck here in this desert drinking hole on December 25th, and because I love you, boy, I want you to know why you and I are here far from home and, far from your mother, to whom I still send those huge cheques that paid for your college and your house on the Wicklow Hills but it's this, this is the story ... "

*

"Before I got drummed out of the RAND Corporation, I saw it, I knew the truth. The truth came in a blinding flash. I felt like St. Paul. I knew there was an answer. I knew there was a ship. I saw it in my mind's eye. I saw it between two stars, a ship circling the universe, you can't see it, you have to believe rather than see. This universe-circling spaceship cannot be detected by any equipment. It is invisible. It is insensible. It is a transcendal spaceship. Transcendental, son. Transcendental. I detected it by running the numbers, by using my mind. My mind has been a terrible burden to me, Son.

"I figured out this invisible insensible transcendental spaceship by running the numbers on the universe and worked it all out, and I presented a paper which was called 'My Christmas Preliminary Plan for a Universe-Circling Spaceship' that postulated, son, which postulated, that there were a group of scientists as old as time itself, who made everything that is, that were, if you will, the uncaused cause. I figure that these scientists in the aforementioned invisible, insensible transcendental spaceship, passed our part of the cosmos on an endless quest for love and truth, and when the moment was right, they gave the word and LIFE evolved as the light from a distant star signals the moment of truth. And those wise and ancient benevolent scientists on that invisible insensible transcendental spaceship, going where only benevolent scientists go, fostering life all over the universe, will be back to take us – all life – back to themselves.

"And I wrote my paper for RAND, published it to uproar from the churches, and the government and the league of indecency and they, all of them, the whole job lot, demanded my resignation and drummed me out of the corporation. I said to them, can you, any of you, disprove the existence of a benevolent scientist-filled universe-circling undetectable spaceship, can you disprove my numbers? 'NO!' I shouted.

"No answer from them yet, and here I am hanging out at this gin joint here at the end of the desert by Area 51, talking to my estranged son whom I miss terribly and I love you, boy – you and I are so alike. I can tell you and I are so alike. You are also cursed with my gifts of thought and cogitation..." And when my father said that I began to cry.

And Dad handed me this paper I read to you now, this paper called "The Christmas 1947 Preliminary Design for a Universe-Circling Spaceship."

HAMBURG WOMAN'S SONG
Philip Casey

Time has gone slowly by the hour,
by the year it has gone like a day
and you and I are of a sudden old.
But behind my bright eyes, papa,

I will always be a girl of ten,
and you, a grown man of twenty
when you cheated the dreaded police
who wanted to take me away.

I was born in a time and place
to a woman I look like now,
but fear grew like mould on bread
in my mother's love for her slow girl.

I remember the sirens and cobbles,
then waking at dawn by a stream
where you left me with a countrywoman
and time went slowly by the hour.

She who was my mother
died in the Hamburg fire,
and he who was my father
never came back from the east.

My hands hardened and my bones grew long.
I trusted what I could not understand
until one morning you came up the road
and happiness changed my face.

I am a woman of Hamburg
who walked to the hungry city
side by side with my new father.
I have lived here to this day.

Community Matters
Clare Scott

Her pure clear voice soars
Alongside trills of throaty flute
And feet press new tracks
Through long-standing fields
To the edge of wild lands
Divided by sea
Crossed by coracles.
Traditions revived for gain
The profit in new lives
Resurrected from embers.

Westerly winds hum gently,
The soft mists caress
Lichen-splashed dolmens
Where ancestors danced
Along torch-flared spirals.
Still pummeled drums
Are calling our tribes
To unified action,
Though battles are over,
Mebhdh and Demeter
Carousing in triumph.

Assembled choirs harmonise
A resonant song
Ringing tones on a mobile
While bees drink deep in clover
Until called to the hive
By the soundless horn
To weave the honeycomb
That sweetens sad lives.
The wireless message states
Balance is everything and
Feeds the land that supports us.

THE SEAL'S FATE
Eoin Colfer

The baby seal looked at Bobby Parrish through round black eyes. Cute if you liked that sort of thing. If you were a girl with posters of sad eyed French kids all over your room. Boys didn't do cute. Boys caught fish and gutted them and fed their innards to the gulls. Boys killed things because that was how life was, and you better be ready for it when school was over. Bobby knew that when Saint Brendan's doors closed behind him for the last time, he would strip off his uniform put on some oilskins and take his berth on *The Lady Irene*.

Still, the seal was cute. Bobby could admit that much to himself, as long as no one was around. He was careful to think it quietly, in case one of his friends was telepathic. The animal's black nose quivered and white sunspots spread across its back like a mane. Cute. But like his father said, it was vermin.

Bobby crawled a couple of feet closer, careful not to startle the seal. Limestone crags pressed into his stomach, and rock pool slime destroyed his jeans. It didn't matter. A working man had to be able to ignore discomfort to get the job done.

The seal watched him calmly. It was not afraid. Quite the opposite, it was excited by the prospect of company. It arched its back, slapping its flippers on the slick rock. Bobby slapped the rocks himself, trying to get a bit of a rapport going. It seemed to do the trick. The seal stretched its tiny head forward, coughing three short barks.

We're friends now, thought Bobby. Buddies. This seal probably thinks we're going to spend the summer swimming around the bay, fighting crime.

Well, old buddy, sorry to disappoint you, but your future is not going to be quite so rosy.

Bobby reached behind him, wrapping his fingers around the club's handle.

*

Dick Parrish had spoken from *The Lady Irene*'s deck. The young people gathered around the quay walls above, hanging on his every word. The men never spoke to the boys down the dock. This must be important.

Bobby thought his Dad was like a different person, surrounded by sea and stone. He was invincible, with wind lines burned into his face, and hands that could strangle a conger eel. Every step he took away from the sea diminished him, until at home he would collapse into the armchair and have someone bring him tea.

But here, he was in his element, and everything about him was fierce.

'It's the seals, boys. They're a bloody plague.'

He called them boys, even though Babe Meara was in the group. Babe considered herself a boy, and anybody who suggested otherwise better have shin guards.

'I saw three today,' cried Seanie Ahern. 'Off the point.'

'There were four!' corrected Séan Ahern, his twin. 'And they were in the bay!'

The Ahern twins would argue about the colour of mud. Their real names were Jesse and Randolph, but who would be mean enough to remind them of that?

Dick raised his hands for silence. The brown palms were crisscrossed with white rope burns and welts. Fishing, statistically the most dangerous profession in the world. Two of his brothers hadn't been lucky enough to get off with just rope burns.

'They're everywhere,' he said. 'The bay, the point, even poking their noses into the dock, the cheeky buggers. They're infesting the entire peninsula this year. A fellow I know from Ross reckons the seals are thriving on all the effluent pumped from the factories.'

The Ahern twins giggled and elbowed each other when they realised what that actually meant.

'I wouldn't mind that, if they'd stick to eating waste, but those seals are eating our catch, and they're ripping the nets apart.'

Everybody knew what that meant. Holes in the nets led to long evenings weaving them back together with sharp twine wearing grooves in your hands.

'Things are bad enough already this year, without having to put up with these vermin too. We haven't had a sniff of a mackerel all summer and the crabs are either getting smart or scarce.'

The other men nodded, muttering their agreement around roll-up cigarettes. Hard times were upon them, no doubt about it. Duncade was just about fished out, what with the factory trawlers and the Spanish boats sneaking into Irish waters. Mackerel had always been the life's blood of the south east, now there were barely enough to bait the pots. There hadn't been a silver sea in years. This was when huge shoals of sprats, mackerel's meal of choice swam along the coast and often into the dock itself. When that happened every man, woman and child was pressed into service, and every container from bucket to laundry basket was lowered into the sea to trap the silver blue fish.

'So, here's the way it's going to be,' said Dick Parrish. 'We're going to fight back. From this day on, there is a bounty on seals.'

Bobby felt a jolt of electricity hop from kid to kid. A bounty meant money, and there is no better way to excite youngsters than the promise of money.

'Anyone who brings in a seal's flipper gets a crisp pound note from me.'

A pound, thought Bobby. That's an entire day's farm wages. Then he thought of something else.

'A seal's flipper?' he said. 'But that means you would have to ...'

'Kill it, son,' said his father flatly. 'Kill it dead with rocks or clubs. I don't care. They are big rats and we will send them packing.'

The others were with him, the combination of bloodlust and riches, sending their hearts racing. Seal bounty had been commonplace fifty years ago. All their parents and grandparents had hunted the rocks for extra money. But there hadn't been a bounty in decades. It was most likely illegal.

'I want you to find those rats wherever they try to sun themselves. This summer you will be waiting whenever they poke their shiny heads above the waves. Waiting with something blunt to smite them. Do you hear me?'

The boys nodded, trying to appear casual before the fishermen. Real men of the sea did not get excited. Moby Dick could breach off his bow, and a real fisherman would spit over the gunwales and pretend not to notice.

'We all know the spots where the seals go. Lure them in with a slab of cod, then let them have it with the club. Take care mind, a bull seal will take a chunk out of your leg with its teeth. Worse still, it will break your bones with a swipe of its tail.'

Bobby felt his heart expand in his chest. He hoped its thumping would not shake his jacket. But he was not ready for all this talk of killing and broken bones. It was too soon. Thirteen years of age. Too young to smoke, but old enough to kill a seal. Bobby glanced around at his companions. Paudie, the twins, and Babe Meara. Their eyes were alight. He tried to match their giddiness, for his father's sake.

His father, standing there in command of the whole dock. Bobby realised that Dick Parrish was a leader to all these men. They looked to him for example. It was a crippling year, and damned if Dick hadn't come up with a solution. His father felt the look and threw Bobby a wink.

Be the first, that wink said. Be the first on the slip with a seal's flipper.

Bobby winked back, adding in a grin, but it felt like a sticker, pasted over his real feelings. He didn't want to kill a seal. He didn't know if he could.

*

The seal's eyes were hypnotic, round and black as though they knew things that you never could. What have you seen? wondered Bobby. Deep ocean chasms? Mysterious tentacled creatures that could swallow a ship? Your family's blood spread across the flat rocks, diluted with every lap of the tide?

'Stop it,' he hissed at the cub. 'I know what you're doing. Trying to make yourself real to me. But it won't work, you're vermin. Nothing more. That's what Dad says, and who am I going to believe? You, a seal I never met before, or my own father?'

Bobby hefted the club. Believe it or not, it was a family heirloom. Bobby's grandfather had used it for general clubbing duties in the first half of the century. Granddad had presented the macabre relic to Bobby when he heard about the bounty.

'I whittled this myself out of a lump of ebony that came off an African wreck. It might be old, but by Jesus, you whack anything living with this and that's all she wrote. See this here ...'

Granddad pointed with a nicotine-browned finger to a splat patch on the club. 'That's from a shark that got caught up in the nets one time. I took one eye out of him and half his brain with a single belt. He survived though.' Granddad had lost himself in the memory, gazing out to sea. Looking at things only he could see. 'He's out there now. Half blind and completely mental. Waiting for me to put so much as a toe in the water.' He handed Bobby the club. 'It's all yours now, boy. Pull well back and follow through. Oh, and wear old clothes. When a seal's bowels go, they go everywhere.'

Bobby ran his finger along the club's grip now. A single strip of hide twisted six inches up the shaft. Granddad claimed to have stripped it from a rhinoceros who ran into his jeep when he was on safari, knocking himself unconscious. The rhinoceros still waited for Granddad in Africa, just waiting for him to put so much as a toe inside Kenya. The strap felt like linoleum to Bobby.

The boy stood and took a step closer. Every step took him closer to the next part of his life. His friends couldn't wait. They wanted to hop into adulthood, grins red with seal blood. Smoking would be after that, then the boats, then weekends in the pub.

Bobby wished there could be a part in-between. Maybe there had been once, but adolescence was being eroded like soft rock. It was straight into adulthood now. No time for acne or moods.

Bobby held the club out in front of him. Pull well back and follow through. The seal followed the club with those damned eyes. It's not a fish, Bobby wanted to shout. I'm going to kill you with this, so stop looking at it like it's your best friend. At that moment, Bobby hated the seal. He hated it for being so stupid and trusting, and for tearing nets.

Bobby took several breaths, psyching himself up. It's an animal, he told himself. Vermin. One blow and it's over. Do it and belong. Don't do it, and be excluded forever.

The seal cub obligingly hoisted itself up on its front flippers, angling its conical head. The perfect target. There would never be a better target. Bobby wrapped both hands around the club, squeezing until the blood left his knuckles. He lifted the club high over his head …

*

It had been Babe's idea to set up a practise area. She was very bloodthirsty for a girl.

'Soldiers train for battle,' she explained, suspending the melon in a home-made string harness from a tree branch. 'So we should get ready to hunt the enemy.'

'Enemy?' said Bobby doubtfully.

Babe turned on him. Her name really didn't do her justice. Babe Meara was cynical beyond her years, and aggressive beyond her size. Several local lads had misjudged Babe's nature and were now walking with limps.

'Yes, Parrish,' she spat. 'The enemy. Seals. You should know better than anyone. Your own Dad's nets are taking the worst hammering. If I was you, I'd be diving off the rocks with a knife, hunting those vermin down.'

It was probably true. Babe had once tracked down the dog who ate her cat. Mister Toodles had been avenged with a half-pound of steak stuffed with laxative pellets.

Babe took a magic marker from her pocket, drawing rough features on the melon. Round black eyes, a button nose and some whiskers.

Seán Ahern was a bit slow to catch on. 'What is that? A cat?'

Babe threw the marker at him. 'No, dimwit. Hello. Seals. We're hunting seals, remember?'

Seán rubbed his forehead. 'Oh yeah, seals. I see it now.'

His brother Seanie chuckled derisively. 'A cat. Dimwit.'

'Yeah, well the nose threw me. It's kind of feline looking.'

Babe set the melon swinging, then backed up half a dozen steps taking a hurl from her belt. The hurl was two feet long with wicked looking metal bands criss-crossing the base. This particular hurl was banned from every playing pitch in the south-east, but Babe kept it around because it had a good weight and you never know when you might have to whack something.

She hefted the hurl like a midget ninja.

'The way I see it, the little bugger is lying on the flat rocks, tearing up a length of net.'

Babe advanced slowly, walking sideways, hurl high behind her.

'So you come in slow. Never taking your eyes off the ball, I mean head. He'll be moving about a bit so you have to try and anticipate.'

Bobby tried to grin along with the rest of them, but he had always had a good imagination. He could see the seal. For him the pale green melon had morphed into a water slick deep brown head. The inked eyes sparkled and rolled. The ragged whiskers shivered in the breeze. The smile on his face was only skin deep.

Babe froze two steps from the target.

'This is the crucial point,' she whispered. 'This is when the seal could spot you. Then the bugger has two choices: He can run, or he can fight.'

She twirled her hurl in one hand. It cut the air with a gentle whoosh.

'So you have to be ready for both.'

With speed honed by years of competition with taller people, Babe Meara took the final two steps, bringing her hurl slicing down at the swinging fruit. The first blow battered the melon from its harness of string. The second shattered it into a million soggy pieces before it hit the ground.

'Jesus,' blurted Bobby.

Babe grinned, green melon juice spattered across her forehead.

'Will you look at him. He can't even stomach someone killing a piece of fruit. You'll never be able to handle an actual seal.'

The others laughed, giving Bobby farmer slaps on the shoulder.

'Go on, Bobby, you eejit.'

'Get a grip, Parrish. It's a melon. You on the other hand are a lemon.'

But Paudie, Bobby's closest friend in the group, went deeper.

'Don't worry, pal. When the times comes Bobby Parrish will show us all. Isn't that right, Bobby. You'll show us.'

Bobby looked Babe in the eye, trying to salvage the situation.

'That's right. I'll show you.'

Babe held out her hurl. 'Why don't you start with a melon?'

*

As it happened, Bobby didn't have to go next. Paudie had grabbed the hurl and made a feck of the whole thing; prancing around, putting on a funny voice. Eventually striking his melon and stamping on the pieces. It was funny enough to make Bobby see that the melon was only a melon, no matter how many features Babe scrawled upon it. When his turn came, Bobby drove the melon right out of its string harness. But it was only a melon, and it proved nothing.

Now things were different. This was a real seal, not a piece of fruit with a shell approximately the same size as a seal's skull. And the seal's head was not swaying in a gentle, predictable arc. It was cocked to one side, staring fixedly at the club raised over Bobby's head.

His father had probably been disappointed in him, though he hadn't said anything. He had not been the first to bring in a seal's flipper. The smart money had been on Paudie, but Babe Meara had surprised them all by backing up her big mouth with action. She arrived on the slip two days later with a brush stroke of red on her shirt and a flipper in her hand. She tossed the flipper onto the flags where Dick Parrish was gutting pollock.

'Pound please,' she said quietly.

Dick handed it over. Babe took it, shoving it deep in her jeans pocket. No gloating. Not a word. Babe went home and no-one saw her for a couple of days. Bit of a chill, her mother said.

So now it was Bobby's turn. He had been doing his level best to avoid seals, but now this little fella had more or less jumped out of the sea into his lap. The hereditary club was raised over his head and there was only one way for it to go. Down.

Bobby could feel the strain in his muscles. It was soon or never. Through the arch of his arms Bobby could see the dock's high wall. There were a couple of youngsters walking along the wall. Picking their way barefoot across the sharp patches of wind scraped rock. When they reached the end, they jumped with squeals and splashes aplenty.

Bobby smiled. He could imagine the cold water folding itself around him. There was no better feeling. That moment of clear touch and sluggish sight. Then back into the world of air.

That's what I should be doing, he thought. I should be diving off the high wall, and hunting for baits and throwing fishing heads at girls. Not Babe obviously. Other girls. Not killing seals.

Kill the feckin' seal! said another part of him. Kill it and don't make waves.

It's vermin. Kill it! shouted Dad and Granddad and Babe and a hundred other voices in his head.

Bobby heard the two youngsters giggling in the distance, as they mounted the wall for another jump. He longed to join them. Throw down his family club, put on his old swimming togs with the anchor on the pocket and join them. But he couldn't. This summer a new phase of his life began. He was a young man now. Certain freedoms came with that but also certain responsibilities. He could stay up to watch action movies, he could cycle the five miles to the local disco, he could even bring the boat out on his own around the bay. But he also had to earn his keep, learn to smoke, and kill seals.

It seemed as though he had been holding the club over his head for hours. The tendons in his arms sang like guitar strings. And the seal cub waited patiently for the game to begin.

I am stuck, thought Bobby. Trapped in this position. I don't want to do this, but I have to.

'You don't have to, son,' said a voice behind him.

Bobby turned, the club still raised above him.

His father was on the bank, squatting elbows on knees. His face was difficult to read. Maybe understanding was there. Maybe disappointment too.

'I do have to, Dad. I can too.'

Dick Parrish shifted his weight. 'I know you can son, but you really don't have to. Look.' Bobby's dad stood, shielding his eyes against the sun. He pointed a finger out into the bay.

Bobby turned seawards, and for several moments could see nothing out of the ordinary. Then he noticed a wedge of light among the wavelets. At first he thought it was a sun shimmer, until it switched directions three times in a second.

'Sprats,' breathed Bobby.

'Yes,' said his father. 'The mackerel are coming in. All hands on deck. Let's go.'

The mackerel were coming in. For the first time in years. He was off the hook, for now. And maybe, if the fish stayed in for a few weeks, the bounty would be forgotten. Bobby lowered the club, glancing down towards the seal cub. But there was only a wet stain on the rocks, evaporating as Bobby looked at it. The seal knew the fish were coming and he would be there to greet them.

Bobby hurried up the rocky incline after his father.

'I'll take the boat out,' said Dick Parrish briskly. 'I want you on the short wall with a line of feathers. Take a fishing box too, you'll need it.'

Bobby nodded. He could fish. Killing fish was easier than killing seals. People ate fish.

'Get your brother down here too,' continued Dick. 'He could do with a couple of hours away from the books.'

'Yes, Dad.'

They climbed over the stile into the quay itself. Nobody was walking anywhere. Everyone was scurrying.

This must have been what it was like before an air raid, thought Bobby. Everyone has a job to do, and maybe not much time to do it in. He took a moment to absorb what was happening before launching himself into the furore.

The quayside was thronged with locals searching for a good spot, like tourists around a luggage carousel. They carried lines and rods and containers of every kind. Buckets, washing baskets, pots and pans. All to be lowered into the spring tide. The sprats shimmered into the mouth of the dock like a sheet of sub-aqua chainmail, and behind them the silver blue flash of a million mackerel, driving themselves greedily towards the dock. Once in, they would be trapped in the simple maze of quay walls, and only the lucky ones would escape.

The locals had about three hours before the tide emptied the dock, then the remaining fish would be piled high on the sand, rotting quickly in the sun. Nobody wanted to eat rotting fish, so they had to be lifted from the water. As many as possible. The beached fish would be shovelled into salt and sold for fishmeal or bait.

Bobby's father clapped him on the shoulder. 'Enough gawking. Get a move on.'

'Right,' said Bobby and set off at a run down the quay. Something made him stop and look back. His father was watching him go with a lost expression on his face.

You are not me, that look said. I thought you'd be a little me, but you are your own person.

Dick Parrish cupped a hand around his mouth.

'Maybe we can talk later, about stuff. You know, girls or seal clubbing or whatever.'

Bobby stopped but didn't look back. His Dad had thrown the invitation out casually, but there was nothing casual about the subjects.

But talking about clubbing seals was better than doing it. Bobby waved over his shoulder, then set off for the yard at a run.

Facepainting
Erin Fornoff

Her mother says maybe
she could be a princess
today, and I knock
cloudy water off a brush
and anchor her tiny chin
with the pad of my thumb.
The boys all want to be lions
or pirates; predators and criminals--
but she is my fifth princess of the morning.
She disregards my thumb
to ask what she'll look like--
we say, So beautiful.
I shellack her perfect face in white
daub hearts on cheeks,
dot a cupid bow mouth in red,
arch flirting brows
and over it all
lashings of Las Vegas glitter.
Sitting this still for this long
is almost unendurable torture –
She's as happy to be free
as she is to sight the gaudy
stranger where her face
should be. She looks at us

to tell her we love it.
Her father shoots me a look
I can't quite meet.
I've tarted up his three year old
like a truck stop hooker
and I wish I had skipped the
Geisha routine and gone
straight for the warpaint
and slicked it thick, the
kind that doesn't
smear with fast-melting ice cream
or an arm wiped across a runny nose.
She asks how she looks.
We say, So beautiful.
I want to say, Honey,
a princess looks however
they tell her.

No rain in the desert
Simone Mansell-Broome

Call it an epiphany, but not
in a good way – revelation of death
not of birth: that man with the Mr Blobby towel
he made you realise it was over.
Raining when you went there too
August not January ... see mirage, ride camels,
camp

by the oasis, watch sunrise over dunes,
a side dish of that Star Wars village. Like them,
you'd stayed in that desert hotel; expecting
sun; windowless, a sheet, one thin blanket,
as they'd planned for heat.
You were ill-prepared,
underpacked for justabovefreezing
Saharan storms.

It's late in the bar outside. This
is what we have in common, apart from us
both being here – we were sold the dream
Lawrence of Arabia, seventeen degrees
or eighteen, no less, and no, it never rains
in January. Maybe light showers.

You came, were surprised, got drenched
and I picture you changing out of wet trousers
swaying in a coach aisle
while, further back, a large man
fellow sopping traveller, does the same
clutching his Mr Blobby towel
her finding it all so distasteful
you having your Damascus moment

knowing it's over. Sometimes holidays help, quality
time, change of scenery,
but sometimes they give you
clarity, focus, that day – that towel.

The Wex Factor
(A translation of this work is available from the author)
Jackie Hayden

Inspector Wexford examined the GOREY details at the crime scene and looked about him with a determined stare in his eyes.

"OILGATE the BALLYMAHON who committed this murder by HOOK or by crook," he said, staring at the still body of a man who had been tarred and FETHARD before being murdered.

Taking the dead man's girlfriend to the KILLINICK before bringing her and her boyfriend Gorman in for questioning, he first told Garda Coyne to abandon the case he was working on and LOCH GORMAN up.

"We've more important matters to attend now than deal with petty criminals like Gorman," he said.

Under COYNE'S CROSS-examination the arrested woman explained that her name was Roche, CLON ROCHE, and that the victims' name was ROSS LARE. She suggested his death might be suicide as he worked as a screen printer, but he'd been depressed lately because nobody would buy his OUL ART.

"I CARNE handle this," she said, before breaking down. "Me and Ross CAIM to this place for peace and quiet. For a while it worked out really well for us. He became a whole NEW ROSS."

Wexford became impatient. "I know it isn't suicide. I think you know more about this then you're letting on," he said to her.

She then produced a photo from her wallet. "That's TAGHMON who did it. His name's TOM HAGGARD. My ex-boyfriend," she said, wiping a SALTEE tear from her CHEEKPOINT.

The Inspector' assistant PIERCE SESTOWN looked at his boss. "I'll CAMPILE a full report, sir."

Inspector Wexford looked away. He didn't like slobs, especially NORTH SLOBS, believing that they THE FAYTHE all sense of polite discipline. But he didn't have TACUMSHIN to say it to his assistant's face.

Instead, he left the station and drove out to Tom Haggard's place, located in the same village where he'd been born fifty years previously.

Parking his squad car and looking around, he thought to himself, "YOLETOWN looks the same." Almost immediately a crowd gathered around the Garda car. Disgusted, Wexford thought to himself, "The people are still the same too. A squad car arrives and FOULKSMILLS around like flies." Ignoring their banal questions he walked through the WHITEGATE to knock on Haggard's door.

Although he invited the Inspector in, Haggard wasn't inclined to co-operate, so Wexford warned him, "I'll take no argy BARGY from you, Haggard." And putting on his handcuffs ENNISCORTHYed him back to the station.

After dealing with the necessary paperwork, the Inspector arrived back in his office where one of his colleagues was busy at his desk.

"You seem to be working ARD, CAVAN? Anything important?" he inquired sarcastically.

Looking up, Cavan moaned, "This is the FORTH MOUNTAIN of paperwork I've had to wade through this week."

Wexford turned to his secretary Eva LARKINS-CROSS who was browsing through a book about The Pied Piper of CAMOLIN she'd bought for her young daughter. When she saw the Inspector had caught her idling, she jumped up and walked hurriedly up the BLACKSTAIRS.

Suddenly she turned and said to him, "I can see who did it. CARNEW?"

"No. I don't know. CROSSABEG you to tell me," he implored her, sneaking a look at the CLOGH.

They had an audience. But Sally ignored him, as did MAY GLASS the cleaner.

Wexford arranged a chat with his crew and issued his instructions.

"I want you TAGOAT this Haggard fella bald-headed. Instead of doing the obvious, try a NEWLINE of enquiry."

Turning, he said, "ARTHURSTOWN at the crime scene, checking the place out. ADAMSTOWN there too, so when you're DUN, CORMICK, go and help him."

To another one of his team he said, "I wish you'd finish that BUN, CLODY, although it doesn't smell as bad as the BREE sandwich you had last week. Then bring Haggard into the interview room."

He looked at his latest recruit Cass, and told his team, "CASTLEBRIDGE the gap between the evidence we have to date and Haggard's alibi."

He was about to continue when he was cut short by

Chief Inspector Brendan HOWLIN down the stairs. "Give it TOOMEY straight, Wexford, I don't care how bad the news is. I can take it as WALLACE the next man."

Wexford filled Howlin in on events thus far. "In a BROADWAY, as far as we can determine, it started with a dispute OVER THE WATER. The victim was feeding the BALLAGH owned by Tom Haggard. Then Ross touched on a CARNSORE POINT, claiming Haggard was only interested in the BALLYMONEY and killed him for it. But we've put him away for the time being, where he won't be able to KILMORE."

Chief Inspector Howlin was delighted. "Well done, everybody. Let's go over to FERNS and KNOCKBRACK a few pints, eh?"

Recycled
Paul Harris

I sighted Elvis once,
in downtown Wexford.
He'd consumed
two tons of hamburgers, hotdogs, donuts,
washed down with
a crate of Coca-Cola.

The King dropped dead at my feet.
I took the wasted rocker's demise as a
warning
to curb my self-indulgent ways.
No more would I overdose on real ale
and all-you-can-eat curry.
Giving up pies, chips, beans, buttered buns,
I put a stop to binging on weekends and
weekdays.

I now visit the gym and subsist on cucumber
and water.
I'm better for it,
I'll kill anyone who disagrees.
Although healthier I am a tad irritable.
Can you blame me? I'm starving.

Since staggering into the twenty-first century,
born again into responsible living,
I've decided to save the planet
by fitting out my kitchen
with a dozen colour-coded bins,
one for cans, another for clean glass,
one for dirty magazines and newspapers.
I won't bore you by naming every bin
but I'm after the set,
one for every skip at the Tip.

Rinsing out mucky jars
and putting plastics into the pink bag
I reconsider Elvis,
re-mastered, re-packaged,
re-incarnated in Wexford,
the King
recycled.

Autumn, in a time of Climate Change
Kevin Connelly

Finally,
released from
the endless rains
of that strange summer
we
are free
to be outside,
once again enjoy nature.
Now,
it is
Autumn here. Everything,
although lovely, is changing.
Look,
the red,
brown, yellow, orange,
all the golden kaleidoscopes
of
leaves are
falling. We love
all, knowing something else
follows.

The Impossible Lasagna
для Joel Thomas Hynes

Dave Lordan

Years later, when I think of him, what rises up is the famous Lasagna. Which he himself cooked and which was such a surprise to the rest of us. No-one would have credited that a bedsit chronic like Jim could even conceive of Lasagna, never mind get around to cooking it. But Jim had invited us all around to his place for that Friday night for a 'dinner party' and it turned out that, despite our sniggering at the absurdity of the idea, he meant it.

I don't remember what the Lasagna tasted like, just the look of it, the part-browned top layer of cheese, appetising and aromatic- real Lasagna. I remember Jim drunkenly pulling the Lasagna out of the oven and holding it up to show off before multiple witnesses that it truly existed. We were already twisted on Buckfast and hotknives, of course. We wolfed down the Lasagna.

I reckon that was Jim's last party. St Vincent De Paul took over shortly after. They gave him shoes and clothes and toothpaste and food – all things which were more or less completely useless to him. But I think they paid his rent too, or at least shielded him from eviction. I knew Ted, his landlord well – it's a small town – Ted was a real schemer and he couldn't wait to get rid of Jim and get new regular tenants in.

Sometimes me or one of the lads would drop up with a flagon or two as a gift for Jim, out of our old fondness and our wish to not see him suffer too badly. The DT's is a hard road.

Jim's eyes, I can't really describe his eyes except they looked at you like a creature lying in wait at the bottom of a poisoned sea. They looked at you like a plague that could make you permanently sad and ill.

Jim's hands were raw and cracked and covered in callouses and blisters. It was hard to avoid shaking hands with him – he was such a friendly, needy drunk – but I did, even at the risk of causing offense. I didn't want to catch anything. Everything about Jim was consumed by disease. *He* himself was a consuming disease. Things became sick by belonging to or associating with him. He had a sick settee, a sick radio, sick T-shirts and shoes, a sick toothbrush for his one remaining sick tooth, a sick old guitar with one string left on that, a sick pair of cheap sunglasses he wore around the apartment, a sick past full of sick memories.

During these visits Jim often spoke to us of a son he had had many years ago, with an ex-girlfriend with whom he had broken up before the child had been born. We had never before heard of the child, nor the girlfriend. He said he was hoping to make contact again with the child, now seventeen years of age. The son was, according to Jim, some kind of international martial arts prodigy. The son was playing for Ireland, Jim said, covered in glory and traveling the world. Jim was waiting for the son to turn eighteen, when Jim would be able to legally make contact with him. This fancy animated Jim greatly, whenever he spoke of it, but weeks could go by when he wouldn't make a mention.

Another thing he told me was that he had stopped shitting. I said that was because he had stopped eating. He said life was much less complicated when you neither ate nor shat.

He spoke of time. He said that he had learned to move around inside time. He said he could travel up and down his own life like it was a bridge. A bridge connecting nothing to nowhere he said. Sometimes he went back to his deep childhood, just to watch himself sleeping as a little boy. This was very calming, he said. He often went to his own funeral too. There was a bigger crowd at it than he would have expected, given all the people he had pissed off over the years and all the snobs there were in our town.

I dreamt last night that I killed Jim, that Ted had given me four grand to beat his troublesome tenant to death with a hammer and so free the flat up for profit. I can clearly see Jim's face gripped with agony after the first blow, his hand on his head and the thick gunk streaming out between his fingers. Then I strike him again, and again, until the job's done.

For some time after I woke up I believed it had really happened and I felt oppressed by my guilt. Never before had a dream made such perfect sense.

Loose Haiku

Maeve O'Sullivan

sunday morning
radio voices chattering
a tulip petal falls…

stained-glass-ceiling
wobbling
in my coffee cup

following me
the matchmaker's eyes
in the photograph

a giant bee
flies by the old man
embroidering…

wondering
what it was all week:
hornbeam tree

at the pier's end
an upturned bell
the silent foghorn

THE DAY OFF
Billy Roche

For some unknown reason – inexplicable you might say – Daly woke up one morning and decided on a whim to take the day off work. Twenty-five years working as a clerk in Lawson and Sons Firm of Solicitors and this was the first time he'd ever been so bold, although God knows he'd often threatened as much.

'Yeah, right,' Crosbie would say sarcastically, fingering his frothy cappuccino in the Coffee Pot Café. 'In your dreams, pal!'

'I will. I'll do it,' Daly would swear.

'When?'

'I don't know. One day … Someday.'

'I'll tell you when,' Crosbie would hiss. 'Never!'

Well, today was the day. His wife – a no nonsense merchant – stirred in the bed beside him and squinted at him sideways through those sly, hooded eyelids as if reading his wayward thoughts. She even muttered something to imply that she had him well taped. He held his breath and stayed perfectly still until she fell back to sleep again, and then, being a creature of habit, he rose up as usual on the dot of seven thirty, shaved and showered and tiptoed down the stairs to the kitchen in his stocking feet. He had his breakfast and made his sandwiches – well, cream crackers actually and cheese and mayonnaise with a few grapes on the side, wrapped in tin-foil and imprisoned in a see-through Tupperware container – along with his usual flask of vegetable soup. He even raided the small change jar for money for his eleven o'clock cup of coffee in The Coffee Pot Café, which of course he wouldn't get to have today.

Upstairs he could detect his wife moving around and he hastily slipped on his slip-ons, gathered all his things together – sandwiches, flask, brief case, jumper and jacket – fumbled his way through the front door where he bundled the lot onto the backseat and climbed into the car with a weary sigh of relief. She'd be coming down the stairs any minute now to face the world. 'What's that smell?' she would have said to him had he been there, referring to his aftershave which she saw as an affectation and an invitation to debauchery. It was a standard joke nowadays between himself and Crosbie behind her back: that and 'Where were you, ye liar?'

Daly revved the engine, let it warm up for a minute or two as was his style, steam rising like mist around the bonnet and sides (which for a while there – well in the beginning anyway – unbeknownst to him, made him the laughing stock of the street), and then he noisily took off out of the quiet cul-de-sac, a slightly comical, diminutive, finicky figure behind the steering wheel. He drove past the corner shop and away, through the streets of the bustling little town, booting down the hill past the side windows of Lawson and Sons Firm of Solicitors where he worked, or in this case – today at any rate – he didn't work.

He was sure people would notice him driving by – Linda from the Coffee Pot Café for one who was busy putting out the outside sign. Green eyes like a cat. 'Meeow', he felt like saying sometimes. What if he did go in there someday and starting purring at her like that as she poured out his coffee? Crosbie thinks, given half the chance, she'd scratch the back off you. God, imagine the inquisition.

'Where did you get those?'

'What?'

'Those marks on your back?'

'Penance for my sins.'

'What sins? What have you been up to? Where were you, ye liar?'

There's Bernard, the faithful messenger from the bank, wrenching up the heavy steel shutters. Bowing, bending, he's in. Oh my God, the dickie-bowed Mister Brown the manager is tied to a chair inside, bound and gagged, beaten and buggered. 'Quick Bernard, get out the Sudocrem. In my office, Bernard. In the cupboard above the … Hurry Bernard, hurry. That's it … Gently Bernard, gently … Oh, Bernard!'… And there's the roving traffic warden, hat tilted rakishly, slyly pretending not to notice a few potential lawbreakers. 'Go on park there, I dare you … Park there you … red-headed bastard.'

Daly drives by, unseen. What's one to do? Bamp the horn? Spit into the wind? Drop the pants and moon? But no, nobody flagged him down, no one waved him in to the side of the road and demanded his passport and licence and the gory details of his final destination.

The town would soon be in his rear view mirror, he couldn't help thinking, as he headed for the brindled countryside: The Swan monument, the Faythe Primary School, the Celtic Laundry, Our Lady's Grotto, The Rocks, the sea and the road to Mandalay... He switched on the radio. Yes, Brendan O'Dowda singing, *La Golondrina*. Lovely. 'To Far Off Lands/ The Swallow Now Is Speeding/ To Warmer Climes ...' Oh dear, there's young Mister Lawson, like the ghost of Christmas past, on his way to work. Did he see? No, too busy at other things. Stop picking, we're not playing today. Phew, that was a close shave! About twelve o'clock it'll dawn on him, the dopey dope! 'Were my eyes deceiving me or did I see Daly this morning, driving out of town to the tune of *La Golondrina*?'

There's that field, full of golden sunlight. And a pheasant, doing his little dance.

*

The seaside! A walk along the beach. Crunch, crunch, crunch, crunch ... Hate that sound. And the feel. Aah ... The seagulls circling and whinging and the tarry whiff of the ocean, marred by the reeking stink of the dry-docked fishing boats. A couple of schoolboys nipping down a sandy avenue, playing truant more than likely. Here's your brother! 'Cut out that smoking, it'll stunt your growth – little midgets going around with brown stained fingers, bad teeth and a smell off your breath.'

The Guillemot Lightship, tied up in the harbour – a maritime museum this weather! How much to go in? A fiver? Go on then. Up the gangplank. Ah me 'earties, them that dies be the lucky ones. A tourist in one's own backyard would you believe? There's no accounting. Crow's Nest first. No head for heights. Don't look down. Look out and up. Windmills on the horizon. And what's that in the distance? Is it? No, can't make it out at all. Well, God knows you were warned. Oh, for twenty-twenty vision. Down into the galley afterwards to peep into the tiny cabins. Miniature existence when you think of it. They lived like monks according to this – the Lightship men! Rosary and everything during Lent, so they say anyway!

Crosbie did a stint out here once. Well not here, out on the sea when the Lightship was ... operational. Off the coast of ... Arklow was it? Boring he said it was. Up to the light to do your watch, down to the galley when it was your turn to cook, into the cabin to read your Louis L'Amour. One fellow who never said a word, another who never shut up and a third lad who was constantly sick over the side. Oh Mammy. Mammy Mammy Mammy ... Mammy Mc-feckin'- Grath ... Never again, Crosbie vowed. But then again it could be said that Crosbie was inclined to be a bit backward about coming forward on the work front. The job in the Banjo Bar didn't suit him he said – the hours were all wrong. The Civil Service was for arse lickers. And before that again, just out of school, he'd been offered an apprenticeship in a men's drapery store down town which had lasted all of three weeks. The manager was a sergeant-major for starters, he explained, and measuring men's inside legs was not exactly Crosbie's forté either. *I Joined the Navy/ To See The World/ And What Did I See/ I Saw The Sea ...*

A few miles up the road Daly went into a pub and ordered a half of ale and a bag of peanuts. The place was in an awful state from the night before – screwed up racing dockets and bits of old newspapers and a mark that looked like someone had dragged a dead body from A to B and back again. Jesus, what went on here? The barman served him, handed him yesterday's soggy Evening Herald and told him to go sit in the corner out of harm's way with the added addendum, 'We're not even supposed to be open yet.'

The barman – who must also have been the owner – was going hither and thither, filling the shelves and calling into what sounded like his wife in the living area at the back of the shop. Daly could hear her distant replies, 'Ask my arse,' being one of them.

'I'd rather not,' the barman muttered to no one in particular.

And then a red faced mariner came in. 'Did I leave a big rope here last night?' he wondered accusingly from the windy doorway.

'Ask herself inside there,' came the answer. ' … If she's done with it!'

The red faced mariner disappeared into the living quarters and returned a few minutes later with his rope intact, mumbled a fond farewell and left, leaving the door ajar after him which Daly took it upon himself to close.

'Did you recognise that fella?' the crouched barman wanted to know, his head appearing like a puppet over the tip of the counter.

'No,' Daly piped.

'Martin Hall. Tug-of-War. No? … He's a whore for ropes, that lad is! Goes through them by the new time.'

Apart from that incident there was no real atmosphere in the place and so Daly drank up and left, bringing the unopened peanuts with him. They'd be missing him at the office round about now. Young Mister Lawson would be inquiring after him. Karen would agree that it was odd: no phone call, no doctor's note, nothing. Twenty-five years and never missed a day. Well, granted, he did go home early once or twice – an earache one day, and a sudden bout of vertigo another. And of course from time to time he'd feel a bit under the weather – colds and flus and the like. But a few Beecham's powders and a hot toddy at lunchtime (old Mister Lawson's remedy) usually put paid to that.

He pictured them all, Karen and Crawford mainly, rummaging round for stuff: a file they couldn't locate, a notice that needed an urgent response. They'd probably ring his home to see where he was. His wife would take the call. Naturally enough she'd jump to all manner of conclusions. Crosbie, the seasoned gambler, would get the blame – try the race track, or the betting shop, or that new snooker hall in the Mall. Or an accident maybe, a frantic search through drawers and dressers for that insurance policy which she'd threatened not to renew. No, Marian Bowles though. Daly had been engaged to Marian Bowles once upon a time and her name was never too far below the surface, dredged up to whip him with in times of trouble. Marian Bowles did this and Marian Bowles did the other thing. 'Go back to Marian Bowles, why don't you,' was the constant refrain.

Crosbie might be hauled in for questioning. And even from the dock he'd play her like a violin. 'What was he wearing when he left the house? You don't know? Did he shave? Shower? Shampoo? Aftershave? Ah, yes, I see said the blind man.' In the end, like an overwound cuckoo clock, she'd put on her coat and go down to Healy and Doyle's Department Store to make sure that Marian Bowles hadn't taken the day off too.

On the way back into town, Daly pulled over to the side to study his favourite field again – golden and glorious as it swept down to the sea. He often fantasised about running through this field with his shoes off. Or walking through it with some woman maybe, hand-in-hand. Not his wife, no. Marian Bowles perhaps. Yeah, Crosbie spying on them from the long grass as the pheasant hecked and hopped and hobbled nearby. Marian Bowles had hinted once or twice when she was going out with him that he wasn't nearly half as adventurous as she'd like him to be. What on earth did she expect him to do to her he couldn't help wondering sometimes. When it was all over between them, with Daly's reluctant blessing, Crosbie decided to tackle her himself, only to get short shrift.

'You're vain, ignorant, self-centred, mean, thick, overweight and ugly,' were some of the reasons she rattled off when Crosbie asked her why she wouldn't agree to go out with him.

'No need for it,' Crosbie complained afterwards. 'I mean a straightforward "I'd rather not," would have done me.'

*

The Pond. Some people called it The Otter Pond, others referred to it as Rainwater, but himself and Crosbie knew it merely as The Pond, as if it was the only one. Daly pulled into the patch of waste ground and with the radio on, he drank his soup. The cream crackers and cheese he'd save for later. What's the time? Eleven thirty three. By rights at this moment in time he should be in – no, coming out of – the Coffee Pot Café. Linda might ask someone about him, one of the young solicitors or the junior clerk, or Karen if she happened to slip across for a croissant.

'He's gone walkabouts apparently,' Karen would tell her.

'Is he now?' Linda was sure to say. 'Mmn ... he's a dark horse.'

Daly had been coming out to The Pond for more years than he cared to remember. It was not officially his neck of the woods of course. In fact Crosbie was the one who had introduced him to it in the first place, when they were both in short pants practically. And although the place was usually frequented by hard cases (who by the way were fairly tribal about their territory), nobody ever bothered them. Chances are they had Daly pegged as a harmless birdwatcher, which somewhere in the depths of his secret recesses he sadly lamented. Or maybe it was Crosbie, who could be described as an unknown entity to say the least: a policeman's son who was big, confident, brash and reasonably wise to the ways of the world.

No, while other interlopers were frowned upon and at times punished – tied to posts, dumped headfirst into the water, shoes taken, chased off with stones, shirts ripped and torn, faces washed and fed with horseshit and God-only-knows-what other form of torture – for some strange reason or other Daly and Crosbie were generally left alone, ignored almost. And so while the locals – Tommy Day and Apache Bryne and the Bradley brothers and all the boys – went (like fugitives from some cowboy film) about their business, Daly and Crosbie would sit hunched on the rock in the sun, taking it all in.

The fact that Daly grew up to become a solicitor's clerk proved to be a godsend for many of these people who were, by nature, delinquent. They'd seek him out at the back of the courtroom to ask him what the judge meant by 'consecutive', and 'concurrent', and 'sub judice'. And even today they still looked for him as their children and grandchildren came before the courts – drunk and disorderly, drunk and incapable, drunk and abusive, drunk and in charge of a bicycle. In fact it was a son of one of the Bradley Brothers who was to turn the unwitting Daly into a sort of a working class hero.

The young man showed up one morning for trial in total disarray – unshaved and shabby with an un-ironed shirt and a rumpled old jacket and his hair tangled and unkempt. Mister Moran, his solicitor, shook his head and groaned at the sight of him as Daly ushered the culprit into a nearby lavatory where he produced a comb and an electric razor and proceeded to brush down the dusty jacket before loaning the lad his green spotted tie. The solicitor was delighted with the transformation and when the accused got off with a warning it was mostly put down to the tie. The following week some other ne'er-do-well asked Daly for the use of it and the same bloke – who should have received six months by right – got off with a light fine and a stern warning. The green spotted tie became something of a good luck charm henceforth with criminals of every shade and hue lining up to wear it.

'What is this green tie business?' a visiting judge was overheard to say to old Mister Lawson one day at the top of the winding staircase. 'Some sort of a secret sect or something?'

*

Daly, hands in pockets, was standing beside the dark pond, watching a curlew and a sandpiper dart and darn. He rambled down onto the pebbled strand to catch sight of a heron wading across the mudflats on its spindly stilts. A hint of rain sent him into the planked makeshift hut where he studied the graffiti: What Are You Looking At? the cracked mirror wanted to know in smeared lipstick. Prick ... Shit ... MINGE ... and SHARON'S MOTHER IS A WHORE ...Very nice!

Daly's wife would have called in the sisters at this stage, all three of them. They'd be planning and scheming and ringing around, despatching their hen-pecked husbands off in different directions to look for him. Crosbie's influence would be brought up and no doubt other episodes recalled. The time Crosbie had to carry him home from the Forester's Reunion might be revisited. Talk about drunk and incapable.

'You were like our Lord on the cross,' Crosbie would remind him later when he disputed the story.

'I wasn't that bad now, Crosbie,' Daly protested, a little ashamed that three pints of Guinness and a half an ale shandy could have got him into such a state.

'I had to carry you up to bed,' Crosbie pointed out. 'Over my shoulder like a sack of spuds.'

'Oh yeah,' Daly conceded.

'Yeah.'

The midday train went rattling by and he had a good mind to do something mad, rise up and put his tongue out at someone or give someone the finger or something; or pull his hat to one side maybe and slouch along like a dribbling imbecile beside it. 'Chu chu train ... Chu chu ... train ...'

It began to rain for real as he hurried back to the car where he ate his cream crackers and drank the rest of the soup and listened to the radio for a while before falling asleep in the back seat. When he woke up the rain had stopped and it was sunny. He got out and scrambled up onto the mossy rock where he sat hunched in the sun in a fashion reminiscent of the past.

'Any sign of him?' one of the sisters would be screeching into her mobile phone at this point in time. In fact all the sisters would be talking simultaneosly, embracing the tragedy for all it was worth. His wife would remain silent however, earnestly preparing for widowhood and secretly hatching her plan to call the children – Damien in London and Doris in an adjacent estate; they'd need to be told before she reluctantly agreed to drag the streams, rivers and local reservoirs.

Daly, prising open the bag of peanuts, began to hatch a plan of his own. He'd need an excuse, a good excuse. For Young Mister Lawson tomorrow, who it must be said was full of his own importance these days, conveniently forgetting that he was once a bit of a rake himself. That was when old Mister Lawson ruled the roost in the office. An old established man – with his 'Daly' and his 'Crawford' and his, 'send the lassie into me this instant.' Young Mister Lawson was constantly in trouble back then: a fight in a dance hall, an illicit affair with a married woman, a drunken escapade or two, rugby songs sung and chanted in crowded taverns and bars. Daly and Karen and Crawford would often line up outside the main office, listening to Old Mister Lawson giving the young man inside a good dressing down.

Recently though, young Mister Lawson had taken to wearing three piece suits in place of casual slacks and jacket, and he proudly sported striped braces of late instead of a buckled belt. He'd gone pale and grey practically overnight. And, as if on cue, he was going bald as well. He ate mints and dined out at lunchtime. He'd even joined the Rotarty Club for God's sake.

'Something came up,' Daly would tell him tomorrow from the mat. 'Something important … Personal.'

'What?' he'd want to know.

'I'd rather not say.'

Young Mister Lawson wouldn't like that of course. He'd make that nasal sound and pinch his lower lip and he'd knock the desk with the first two knuckles of his right hand and murmur, 'Fair enough, ask Karen to come into me,' as if he was going to run the matter by her before meting out the necessary penalty.

Daly wouldn't mind but young Mister Lawson was only a wet day in charge. In fact it was Daly who first happened on the dead Old Mister Lawson, sitting upright like Buddha on the toilet bowl with his glasses askew, a magazine on his lap, and his pants down around his ankles. Daly couldn't believe it at first. He called out to him, reached in and tipped him and everything, which was odd because the dead man's eyes were wide open. And then, weighing up the situation and realising that the first one on the scene would be the one who'd come in for most of the hassle – ringing the ambulance and the doctor and the police and explaining it all to everyone, maybe even becoming involved in cleaning up the old man, pulling up his trousers and all that that entailed – Daly, his heart pounding, decided on a different course of action. He'd pretend he never knew. With that thought in mind he closed over the toilet door and a few moments later he was peeping into the outer office to inform Karen that he was taking an early lunch, and he grabbed his coat and slipped down the stairs and across the road to The Menapia Hotel, where they'd never think of looking for him. When he got back it was all over.

Karen was crying into a rolled up handkerchief on the landing and Crawford was on the phone to young Mister Lawson, and the police and the ambulance and the doctor had been and gone. Daly acted shocked and horrified, hugging Karen and comforting Crawford, and when young Mister Lawson arrived he shook his hand and sympathised with him, and when the young man had left, he took it upon himself to shut up shop early and give everyone the rest of the day off.

Crosbie made him tell the story several times, interrupting him on and off and plying him with questions. What magazine was the old man reading at the time, and what page was open, and what kind of an expression was he wearing? Daly answered as best he could, feigning distaste now and again while secretly enjoying it all, particularly when Crosbie made him retell how he had closed over the toilet door, grabbed his coat and left them all to their fate. Crosbie said it put him in mind of the night porter from the Menapia Hotel years ago who could sleep with his eyes wide open, hence inadvertently scuppering the wily plans of small time con men and randy commercial travellers. What was his name? Benson! Or Fenton? Something like that.

Daly stood up and stretched, looked around and embraced the rain-drenched wilderness. He must do this more often. He should have done it before in fact! Pity Crosbie hadn't tagged along really, for old time's sake.

'I'd keep out of his way for the rest of the week if I was you,' Karen might advise Daly as she'd pass him in the corridor the following morning. 'He's not that happy with you at all, you know … Where did you go anyway?'

'Ask my arse,' Daly would feel like saying to her, but of course he wouldn't.

In the centre
Chris Ozzard

in the centre was a green arc
a blue triangle placed therein
pointed downwards led to a beam
of blue light that transcended sense

– you touched the paper of the map
and the blue light coincidentally moved
so that when your fingers touched again
your key light activated it into neon blue,

that burst through a porthole window
in the unearthly gloom where bright vermillion
pods of OCEA Neptune labs are sited
emblazoned with flags waving from aerials:

– you are on an island, an unattractive
small landmass, turbulent seas
and weather and isolation force all to shelter;
little dwells here except molluscs and Crustace:

except at the knoll on Zemminski's Peak,
south facing terraces harbour extremely rare
Alpine flora, snowbells and Myriad beetles -
(living fossils), figwort gentians (timeseeds)

– nights' dominion bring aurora borealis
in deep hemispheric blue or red bars
over the few stormless nights whales
sing and narwhals pirouette in your dreams

conjured by the island's magnetic disturbance
from bolometric ironstone in magnetite cliffs
below a lightship for shipping, beyond satellite beacons
warn of wrecks circling the island as a danger zone

– few humans have ventured here, unless forced
by science or maritime pursuits and only then
under extreme duress, Bosford abandoned it
as a small penal colony in C19th for the most heinous…

Then at the turn of the new millennia scientists
discovered energised protons cascading from the sun
through the earth's celestial body, at no other
point on earth. The island appeared as a vessel:

A Vessel of Absorption, they called it, into which
protons stream in a tornado-like funnel. Why?
What attractors or aspect of attraction is there?
Why when other Treons fall like rain through Earth,

do these protons spin into this vortex? Into this hole,
into this unobservable until now phenomena. It captures
and disturbs the whole scientific community on Earth?
Are they all protons – or are these Treons ions?

Actively attracted into this still point, the Earth's eye,
this ugly black island amid its tortuous seas? Stationed
for a mere six weeks scientists and fellow support
staff bolster an active population on the island to 226.

In two years 16 people have lost their lives
and 7 are yet unaccounted for. Lost at sea, cliffs
or as in the case of Aijya Narathupolloga (28)
she vanished after returning home to Vermont?

Most of the work is citing beacons and sensitive
recording apparatus, monitoring, and maintaining
the invisible dome of digital beams built over the isle.
On March 21st 2003, an extreme solar flare erupted

& the Treons cascading from the flare increased
beyond measure – this was known as Rupture Z7.
In the 4 days before Rupture Z7 reached Earth
the island was abandoned in fear of excess Treons.

US satellite Bivouac 4728 monitored the Treon vortex.
Weather systems erupted over the planet, causing
numerous storms, and at one point 3000 lightening
sprites where recorded sparking over the ionosphere.

In the North Atlantic a gigantic hurricane nicknamed
Rubin headed toward the Kasparov Island chain – to
limit possible damage a Soviet/NATO force was launched
to cloudseed Rubin's perimeter and to change its course.

Change course it did, Rubin fragmented south, seeding
disturbed weather systems that may have inevitably
led to later hurricanes such as Katrina (cf New Orleans).
Rupture Z7 produced vast Treon activity and disturbance.

The recorded speed of a Treon
is approximately 0.378 light years per second,
or 1,360 light years per hour - the speed of 1 light
year* is equal to 300,000 kilometres per second.
*(On the 30 June 2004 the speed of light was found to be incorrect.)

The density of Treons, or energetic proton particles
fragmented local radio, defence systems & satellite
stations across the globe along with the X-class solar flare.
On the island a recovery party found all destroyed.

In June 2009, a reclamation team was sent
recovering many of the scientific equipments
and naturalists returned to the terraces on
Zemminski's Peak only to discover the Myriad beetles

had increased in size to 15cms, and that other....

I WOULD LIKE TO INTERRUPT THIS POEM
WITH A WARNING:

"GO HOME
GO HOME NOW ... "

Watermarks
Suzanne Power

All your life you feared water.
A hiker on a headland saw you
floating face down on the bay side.
Before you met the open sea
you were found.
Brought out of the cold.
I heard it on the news.

Someone suggested
That it might be you
Not in water we said.
You were afraid of baths.
Washed all your life
in a scullery sink.
You were missing days
before your wife phoned.

She claimed your body.
Your skin on a slab.
Hard man. Rogue. Full back.
No one in that room knew how to cry.
My sister said it was a shrieking sound.
She phoned to say I had lost a hero.
You were brave. The only thing
I told anyone that night

I lit a candle to your truthful days,
Felt you were in what was left.
Locked in the ribs, listening.
Ready to let them have it.

When I got to you they had made you clean.
You were in a box for the first time.
There were bruises. Watermarks.
Honest as you had been.
The only young thing left.

They talked about your appearance.
As if the marks were not there.
He's like he used to look before.

The hardest thing.
Wanting to know what it was
for you to go under.
Did you rise against the choice?
Did you try to change it?
Watching the dark pier slip away
with your own life?

The mourners kept to the edge
Of events.
Sitting by your open casket.
Pooling stories of you as you were.
Talking of anything but this.
It's easy to drown that way.

Watermarks
Suzanne Power

All your life you feared water.
A hiker on a headland saw you
floating face down on the bay side.
Before you met the open sea
you were found.
Brought out of the cold.
I heard it on the news.

Someone suggested
That it might be you
Not in water we said.
You were afraid of baths.
Washed all your life
in a scullery sink.
You were missing days
before your wife phoned.

She claimed your body.
Your skin on a slab.
Hard man. Rogue. Full back.
No one in that room knew how to cry.
My sister said it was a shrieking sound.
She phoned to say I had lost a hero.
You were brave. The only thing
I told anyone that night

I lit a candle to your truthful days,
Felt you were in what was left.
Locked in the ribs, listening.
Ready to let them have it.

When I got to you they had made you clean.
You were in a box for the first time.
There were bruises. Watermarks.
Honest as you had been.
The only young thing left.

They talked about your appearance.
As if the marks were not there.
He's like he used to look before.

The hardest thing.
Wanting to know what it was
for you to go under.
Did you rise against the choice?
Did you try to change it?
Watching the dark pier slip away
with your own life?

The mourners kept to the edge
Of events.
Sitting by your open casket.
Pooling stories of you as you were.
Talking of anything but this.
It's easy to drown that way.

I watched your lips busy in life.
Thin and done.
You looked small for one of my heroes.
Say something,
I asked the place you still occupy.
You never did what you were told.

Your closest brother requested
a minute alone.
Before they closed you in.

At the grave a passing heron took your
Indian spirit while we sang,
It's all over now, baby blue.
We followed one another to a shabby room.
In all the things they spoke of then
You were not mentioned.

Outside in a sky full of rain
I saw you swimming the watermarked clouds.
Free of the talk you once loved.

Mare Rubrum
Helena Mulkerns

She was awakened slowly by the sound of no sound. Or almost none. Turning over, slipping back towards sleep, it was the early hour that she usually awoke, but the roar of the MiG jets was absent. Every morning for weeks now, in the capital, she had been woken by that incredible scream of burning fuel that distinguished the take-offs of the nation's fighter planes.

She threw the sheet away from her and lay on her back, trying to evade consciousness. There was a sound though – muted and repetitious, it inspired rest; complimented this state of half-sleep. She relaxed again, and returned to it after a while with slow recognition: the sea. The creep of water up a beach, the neat slap of tide against the sand, and the swirling, mellifluous drag backwards, to meet the next surge. The relief of a day without the bombs and dust of the city made her not want to waste it. She pulled on a pale linen dress and her hat, and grabbed a towel.

The door dragged along the stone floor as she tried to open it, pulling in sand that had scattered across the verandah in the night. Its wood was old and warped, almost no paint left to speak of, since the hotel had lain vacant during the decades of war. A jumble of roses had grown wild over the filigree woodwork of the balcony and in an open sky, the sun was ascending from the horizon of a calm, blue expanse.

There was a forsaken enchantment to the early morning beach. *Mare Rubrum* – the Red Sea. She walked down and sat a few feet from the waves, imagining the galleys that once sailed past, bringing spices and silks to Rome from India and China. How many wars since then? She watched the strengthening light shimmer like liquid across the surface of the water, gradually feeling the heat build on her shoulders and head, let her hands rest on her knees.

After some time, out of the corner of her eye, she became aware of a figure walking slowly in her direction along the water's edge. The blond head indicated another foreigner. About ten feet away, a man stopped and smiled, crooking his head, as if requesting her approval to approach. She smiled back, not moving. He walked slowly over, bent down silently at her side and stretched forth his two hands, offering something within. She looked. In his right palm was a tiny green and black starfish, droplets of salt water on its strange, intricate patterns, glistening in the sun.

She was completely captivated. He gestured for her to hold out her hand, and placed his gift into her palm.

"For you."

She looked at the starfish, then at the man, who was watching her and smiling. "Beautiful?"

"Yes, beautiful!" She was fascinated by the creature, its convoluted design and its vibrant, watery life. Shades of gold, black and lime all shimmered from its tiny form in the light.

The man's eyebrows crinkled into a sort of quizzical arch, and he looked as if he was trying to determine whether to stay or go.

"Thank you." She smiled, and then again more broadly when he sat down. His hair, close up, was more silver than blond, and his eyes were riveting in their intensity, relaying a blend of scepticism and happy surprise, as if he were as astonished to find her as she was to see him.

It was evident that he spoke almost no English, although he was willing to make the most of what he knew.

"Beautiful!" he said, indicating the sea in front of them.

"Waves," she said.

"I love. Always."

"The oldest sound."

"Yes," he said. "But also new. Every time new. And new and new and new…"

He said this with drawn-out, somewhat grandiose emphasis, echoing the movement of the surf with small gesture of his hand and head.

"You are from Russia?"

"Hmmmm … something like that," he said, grinning as if challenging her to guess. From one of the post-soviet independents, then.

"You are English?"

"Nothing like that!" she said, mimicking him.

"Ha! Irish…" He seemed chuffed at the joke, and they shook hands in a conspiratorial bargain.

So, he was one of the pilots on the United World carrier flights. The crews based in Khartoum rented cabins in the hotel on a long-term basis. They piloted old Russian Antonovs mostly, transporting anything from supplies, aid workers, military, refugees and often, according to rumour, armaments. He didn't seem like a typical military man, but that didn't mean much. She had given up trying to define people out here – in the field you just never knew. In any case, right now he was just a guy in a bathing suit, with a great face and a skewed sense of joy that she did not care to find fault with.

They left the starfish on her towel and walked along the beach. Communication eased into a blend of mime, gesture and noises as well as speech. He had a habit of repeating words a couple of times in succession in order to emphasise them, and he didn't seem to tire of trying to make her laugh.

"I drive plane!!" He indicated this with full visual embellishment. "Where?"

"Khartoum – Juba. Juba – Khartoum. Lokichoggio … Darfour … The nice places, yes?"

"Lovely!"

"Where you want to go, Madame – Hawaii?"

"Zanzibar."

"Sure. For you – first class. Vodka: free, free, free – no question asked!"

"No question asked!" She was delighted. "Frequent flyer miles too?" He grinned back, not comprehending.

After a late breakfast of sugary black tea and flat Arabic bread with honey in what passed for the dining room, they set out to walk along a ghost promenade nearby.

When there were no words, they walked in a pleasing silence. When it got too hot, they went for a swim. The biblical sails of some wooden dhows, ancient as the sea itself, bobbed back and forth in the distance, and every now and then she caught sight of military trucks making their way up the long coast road from the airport. But besides that, they were alone. They went to her room to shower, and stood in a besotted embrace beneath the near-cool water before moving to the bed. It wasn't a difficult progression. He caressed her face with his hand, crinkling his eyes, pronouncing, "beautiful!" They spent the rest of the afternoon under the whirr of the ceiling fan, closing the shutters to deflect the intensity of the daytime heat.

She surfaced somewhere around five, and watched him in the muted, fading light as he slept. He wasn't young, and in fact quite a bit older than his frame initially suggested, and he bore the deeply-lined kind of face that had once been striking and even handsome, but had lost its way somewhere along the line. It was the face of a junkie, an actor.

When he knocked on the door later to pick her up for dinner, he wore plain khaki pants and an old-fashioned waistcoat, adding a somewhat surreal touch of Graham Greene to the evening. And why not, she thought, armouring her head against the mosquitoes with her cream sun hat.

They walked through a maze of narrow, winding streets lined with whitewashed walls. In the absence of street lighting, sporadic haloes of oil lanterns illuminated the craggy faces of men in conversation on the steps of carved wooden doorways. Smells of spicy frying came from a myriad of hidden courtyards and above them, minarets and crosses alternated against the sky.

In a small plaza at the meeting of three streets near the harbour, they found seats at one of four tables lit by a string of low-watt bulbs slung overhead. They ate fresh white fish that had been brought in that day on the boats, served straight off an open fire. Lemon juice and bottled water accompanied the meal, since the fishermen did not serve alcohol. Every now and then, perhaps to bolster Hiberno-Slavic relations, he poured an inch of potent vodka into their tumblers, adding an illicit edge to the meal.

A three-quarter moon had risen by the time they made their way back to the resort to play at being lovers: no better game. The usual little questions bubbled under the surface: family, future, past. She bet he knew the current going wholesale rate for a functional AK47, but why on earth would she ask.

A fog horn sounded out in the bay – the port was still partially functional, but like the whole country, its potential had never been fulfilled due to the conflict, and it struck her that living here sometimes felt like heaving through the last days of a cancerous patriarch, who was strangling his own children in death's throes, and dismissing the nurse from the room as he rasped.

He told her patchily that he was flying back to Khartoum the following morning, and was then set to commence a new run somewhere in Chad, but not looking forward to it. No kidding.

She pushed him back on the pillow and tickled him in the ribs; things were getting far too serious. They were a little less coordinated this time around in their lustful attentions, but the random magic was still there.

Her sleep was fitful, and despite the ceiling fan, she was too warm. Abruptly waking at one point, she was filled with that unnamed anticipation, briefly waiting for the usual roar of the war planes, and relaxed again when the amazing calm of the night kicked in. He had felt her moving, and stroked her face.

"Every morning, in the capital, at this time – there is the sound of MiG jets taking off. They always wake me," she explained.

"MiGs? I drive!"

She waited a moment, not sure she understood what he meant.

"You fly MiG jets?"

"Before."

"Before where?" She hadn't meant her tone to come out like that. He hesitated a moment, sensing the change in her voice.

"Afghanistan…"

She sat up in the bed, and drew her knees under her chin.

"Before, long time…"

"Ah." She couldn't think of any way to respond, and just stared through the mosquito net into the darkness.

"Long time…"

He turned his back to her and rolled on his side, facing out towards the sea, in silence. When she lay back down, he didn't turn to embrace her. She didn't touch him.

She considered this stranger: funny, generous, and if a little worse for the wear and tear, one she had felt comfortable with. Earlier, as she had watched his face in sleep, there was something about it that admittedly, she had half hoped would never be explained.

And yet. Here was a man who gave her a starfish on a beach at dawn.

No more and no less. Enough, maybe. She thought of how they'd found the starfish on the way back home from dinner – where she had abandoned it earlier on the towel at the water's edge. They'd returned it to the sea, but inevitably, it was dying; its verdant colours bleaching down to faded ochre.

She pulled up close to him again, and reached her arm around his chest to hug him. He took her hand in his and held onto it, and they stayed like that until they slept again.

*

It was around dawn when he lifted the white net carefully, and slipped outside it, pulling on his clothes and shoes. She feigned sleep. Before he left, through the mosquito net, he kissed the back of her hand, and she felt the star of his breath on her skin as the door of the room closed behind him.

She listened to the waves through the open window, to this sound they both loved, apparently; the oldest sound, but also new, and new, and new…

Lines Inspired by Flamenco Sketches
Tom Mooney

Night ends
Dawn breaks
Rosy fingered

Moon light
And whale song

After Trojan troubles
The dead inherited the earth
But our motley crew
Of the heroic and the humble
Risked the tribulations
Of a long voyage at sea.

Ithaca
Our home under skies cerulean
Not the glowering gunmetal grey of these days
The curved turban-heads of the vacant and vagrant cloud
And bulbous mists which shoal on anthracite sheets
By sniffing the air, we circumnavigate with care
Until a southerly gale
Dispersed the matted canopy
And unveiled an island

A gleaning cicatrix
A pre-Eden
Verdant and golden

For the first time in nine days
Green came from blue

A surf crashed on a speck-less beach
Screeching gulls soared and dived

We dropped anchor
And our rafts scurried on the swell
Drifting
Lost in thought
Aimless
Doused by fatigue

Our feet took root in the warm sand
Some fell to their knees to give thanks
To wrathful gods who both hound and champion us
For they had provided deliverance
When all we had known was entrapment
Pitched without sail on a darkening whorl

Colours unknown to the eye bathe this new world

Kingfisher scales segued by vermilion dew

I colori sconosciuti all'occhio bagnano questo nuovo mondo
Le scale del martin pescatore segued da rugiada vermilion

The island was a cathedral of green
Encircled by a chrome atoll
Fresh as melting glacier water
Cascading from heights immeasurable to the eye
Ambushed by vibrating lines of golden gossamer
Threading strands of the most luminous green algae
From which hung iridescent pearls of honey
This was terra incognita: paradise bypassed by time
Disregarded by the shifting tectonic plates.

Under
Sparkling foliage
We saw the breeze choreograph the light
Which scattered prismatically.

We bathe languorously in the fluorescent current
Offering private votives
To the azure hall of worship
Cadaverously joyful

At the close of the day, the sun splintered
And from the hibernation of the forest closet
Emerged a tribe of the night, like blind ants
Deft but as silent as the creep of fur
Unselfconsciously naked, earthen brown skin
Backlit by the illusion of radiance
Their arms groaned with magnificent gourds
Over brimming and over spilling
With distilled lotus fruit
And soon
In a monsoon of lust, our cups runneth over

Pleasure
Weightless
Timeless

Ochre suns
Spin silken

Feather light rain in
Thin metal tears sprayed
Our cardboard faces on string

We chased paper cut out hummingbirds
Faced five-foot waves on the reef
And corralled terracotta sea horses into a lagoon

Pelagic birds sang a choral tableaux
All the while we downed the lotus mead
All the while love making
In the erotic lassitude of the distracted
With our Nubian hostesses
Nudes clad only in obsidian necklaces
Beguiling our memory into an ebbing echo
The wildness of our hearts tamed in their hands

The boughs of the orchidaceous trees
Held traceried windows, so slightly ajar
We sauntered into an endless corridor

The lamenting song of the whale

Shall we not wander more?

Or drift in fields of asphodel
Catatonic in a mildewed landscape

Anchored in a vapour of wild sage, blueberry and oregano

We have launched our boats of persimmon bark
Among the peaceful apathy of Andean lakes

Our memory landscaped
Contoured and obliterated
Our tears and our breath impotent
In the eldritch meld of our dreams

Fettered to the vertiginous sea
An archipelago
Of saturated colours

The island was our portal to
A safe haven
From the scarified textures
Of the sea

I journey still
But it's a mystery to me

Asylum

Margaret Hawkins

The journey to the asylum took several hours. The carriage rattled over the rough roads between New Ross and Enniscorthy, the horses finding it difficult to gain speed as snow began to fall and the sharp east wind whipped round them.

'Not a day for a journey like this,' said one of the RIC men as he tightened his uniform under his chin. Only for this he would be back in the barracks in Wellingtonbridge, his behind firmly planted in front of the fire and dare anyone shift him.

The sound of the voice startled Rose. Her head felt heavy and she could remember little of the journey up to now. Where were they? Where were they going? She stirred, trying to look out the window nearest her.

'We're near Boro Hill, missus – we're making good time in spite of the weather.'

The words sounded foreign, the voice distant from her, mixed up with the sound of horses' hooves and the clatter of iron wheels on the roadway.

The other man from the workhouse appeared to be sleeping, sitting opposite.

Rose felt dizzy as the coughing began again. She struggled to search for a rag in her pocket but couldn't – her hands were tied. Panic washed over her, worsening the cough.

The policeman opposite rummaged hurriedly for a rag from the pile under the seat and threw it in her lap at the same time as he and his colleague covered their noses and mouths with their hands.

'This job doesn't pay well enough for what we have to put up with,' thought the second policeman. 'You could catch anything on this job.'

At least the man had been sedated before he left the workhouse so he was giving no trouble. The woman was quiet too but you never could tell. You never knew the minute her kind would lunge at you like a mad cat, eyes spitting fire and nails ready to make red tunnels in your face. It had happened before.

'Doesn't look very robust, though,' he thought. 'The master of the workhouse might have been better leaving her where she was – what are they going to be able to do for her in the asylum in her state?'

The woman hadn't spoken on the journey. Once she'd come to, having fainted as they left the workhouse, she sat in the carriage, her shoulders hunched, her eyes closed or looking vacantly into the distance.

The first policeman was glad of the silence when the coughing bout finished. He wondered what the woman had done to be committed. 'Loose with her favours, maybe – she wouldn't be the first, or the last, who got locked up for that.'

She must have been a fine-looking woman in her day, though, he decided, his eyes darting from her head to her toes. Even leaving the workhouse, she stood her full height, some semblance of dignity in the way she carried her body. Her eyes were dull now, though, and sunken in her head.

Melancholia – how many had he seen with that? He shrugged; wishing asylum deliveries weren't part of his work.

*

'Kilcarberry Mills coming into view – we're nearly there, thanks be to God.'

The male patient moved in his sleep, turning towards his minder as the carriage rounded a bend into the town of Enniscorthy. The policeman shifted position, wary of the man waking, but settled when his breathing fell into evenness once again.

The second policeman was now looking out the window. 'The Slaney – no swans under the bridge today,' he said to his colleague. 'Must have had a bit of sense and gone somewhere warmer for the winter.'

'Aye.'

The carriage made its way across the bridge, slowing to let other traffic pass, then swung right for the Wexford Road.

'Another few minutes. A hot cup of tea'd go down well now.'

'Aye.'

Rose opened her eyes, panic rising in her chest, their movement unsettling her. The madhouse ...The policemen were sitting up and straightening their uniforms now, looking out the window.

The horses' hooves covered another quarter mile of ground.

'At bloody last – the red brick!'

'Lord preserve us from madhouses,' said the other, blessing himself.

'Fine building, though, whoever designed it. Best site in the town too for making an impression.'

'For putting the fear of God into people, you mean.'

Madhouse. Red brick ... Rose began to whimper like a child as the horses started the steep climb up to the entrance. She was outside her body again. 'Hail Mary, full of grace, pray for us sinners now and at the hour of our death...'

The policemen said nothing, disturbed by her muttering.

'Whoa!' The drivers reined the horses to a halt, froth at the corners of the animals' mouths now and sweat visible on their coats after the long journey.

The RIC men unlocked a door each and blew on their fingers as they stepped out onto the snow-covered ground, their warm breath visible in the cold air.

'Out!' The first policeman shook the man in the carriage and pulled him outside. The man staggered, then stood, supported by the policeman.

'Where am I?'

'Come on!' The second spoke more gently to Rose, persuading her to step down.

'Hold onto her, for God's sake,' said the first policeman, going ahead with his charge, who occasionally had to be righted from a stagger. 'I'm not running after anyone on a day like this.'

'Hmph! She won't run far – she's not fit to.'

Rose felt herself being half lifted, half pushed along. The wind caught her breath as she walked the ground, making her gasp, then cough.

The policeman let her go until the coughing ceased, turning his head away from her.

I'll go ahead with this one. He's dead weight with the doping,' called the second policeman.

'Right.'

Eventually the coughing stopped and Rose opened her eyes to look at her surroundings. She felt like a speck beside the huge red brick building. 'Lord help me!' she said.

'You'll be all right. Come on!' said the policeman, anxious to get her off his hands. 'At least you'll get three meals a day here – more than you got in that other place ...'

The clerk's nib scratched as it made the entry in the admissions' register. Rose Murphy. From New Ross Union.

you asked if the cold weather reminded me of home

Sarah Maria Griffin

golden gate park at nine in the evening come a fresh september
has air the texture and shade of a dirty goldfish bowl
an underwater quality all blue and dense
this fog is my country's breath
rolling in and reclaiming me with its grey whisper
cool tendrils all on my bare limbs like tentacles
belonging to a beast from the belly of the ocean
who re-claims girls who ran away from their homes
leaving them on beaches, skirts torn, salty hair
i can hear its whisper in the thick wet air

stall it back to the land where the rain doesn't stop, child
your new freckles have no currency, you do better in the cold
i'm not sure who you thought you were, running off like that
i forgive you, let me hold you, let me hold you, let me hold you

i hear it and i unwind myself,
unpeel the dampness from my skin
stepping into the taxi before i close the door i sing
i am sorry but i am not going with you, dear fog,
i am not going back there again

Mary's Bar
Dominic Williams

The woman waits ...
she is eight thousand years born and has flowed through
Laurentide floes. A sage and a seer, nursed a thousand
siblings of a species long since displaced. A sacrificial
spouse cracked open a womb that spewed East but
migration matters no more, the stars navigate no longer,
supernovas but moments, foretelling the arrival of a significant
one for the land to welcome home her sun-kissed litter

The vessel now at shrunken rest, matriarchal in urban
anonymity. Within a gift, a symbol veiling an epistle
marks this rebirth. An installation water-sealed
and hard knuckle woven. Tough branches of
rebellion bent and interlaced to bear
 safe, a positive force, the power of
a creative thought consummated
 at this predetermined time
this predetermined place

The Berber flees unsettled and unsure
carrying his name in his heart, an isthmus.
Looking for land,
sailing mechanically propelled, pursued by lens and light
to a darkened alley destined to document his significance.
From the south, brushing shores, superficial trade.
An unknown return, man laid naked, epiphany
and she who has waited dances as a child.

WOBBLE

Paul O'Reilly

We're under the bridge drinking the last of the cans when Connors pipes up, 'So will we rob Doyler's bike then?'

Reilly bites, 'Su ... sure what diya want his bike for anyway?'

'Ta ride off into the sunset,' says I, trying to sound like John Wayne.

'Ta sell,' says Connors, 'ta sell ya eegit ya.'

Reilly thinks about it, takes a sup and it's like his head is about to wobble off his shoulders he has it so bad.

'Ta who?' he tuts, his eyes closed from trying to get the words out.

'I dunno,' says Connors, shaking his can and there's only a sup left. 'How 'bout yer sister?'

'I reckon she's good for a ride already,' I jumps in.

'Fu ... fuck off you,' stutters Reilly.

'How 'bout the bike shop then?' says Connors, laughing.

'Wha ... what about it?' says Reilly.

'They sell second hand yokes don't they?'

Reilly thinks about it, watching the muck-red river.

'Would they take his sister?' says I.

'Now fu ... fuckhead, I'm wa ... warning you,' says Reilly, pointing the finger with no nail on it.

Connors waits till Reilly's settled before saying,

'We might get more for her than Doyler's bike all the same Whistler?'

'Now fu ... fucking fuckface,' says Reilly, giving Connors the finger this time.

Connors laughs, sups and throws his can in the river. With the tide on the way out it's gone in the flash. He stands, straightens the trousers a few sizes too big for him.

'I'm going to look for Doyler anyway,' he belches out. 'Are ya coming?'

I look to Reilly but he's still watching the river, his head bobbing up and down now.

I stand, slap the dust off me arse and fasten me coat.

'Are ya coming?' Connors says again.

But Reilly doesn't stir.

Uptown meself and Connors spot Doyler's bike outside the baker's on Church Street.

'I tauld ya,' says Connors, 'he's fond of the éclairs so he is.'

'A right gob on him for the éclairs,' says I.

Connors runs down the path. I keep watch on the corner. He takes a quick look inside the shop, hops on the bike and pushes off singing, 'Raindrops keep falling on me head.' He tears down Church Street and I lose sight of him when he turns down Castle Hill. I run a few steps but me heart starts pumping so fast I can hear it and it feels like the top of me head'll burst if I don't soon stop.

*

There's a crowd gathering on the little roundabout at the bottom of Castle Hill. The traffic's stopped. The bike's lying this side of a Ford Focus and it's like Connors thought he was Evil Knievel but forgot to put up the fucken ramp. Someone says: they should call an ambulance. Someone else says: they should call the guards.

Reilly waddles out around the crowd, walking the way he talks, heading for the bike. He stands over it, whistling the way he can, like a bird on the bridge wall at the crack of day. The wheels still spinning he lifts it, fingers the chain, wipes the grease in his trousers. He pumps the brakes, presses a thumb on each tyre. He looks it up and down and when a trucker from behind blows Reilly ignores it, like he can't even hear it.

'Reilly,' I shouts, starting to run down the rest of the hill, holding onto me chest. 'Hauld on there.'

But Reilly throws the leg over and pushes off, jigging along down to the quay, himself and the handlebars wobbling away from me.

The Need for Leadership
Ross Hattaway

We often enough
in our gentle political discourse
talk airily of leadership
and its need,
as if it is something
that can be plucked
from the air
or tried on like new trousers –
leadership as fashion statement –
in line with the rest of our aspirations.
Today we give
Mandy, 17, from Rush,
who wants to work with animals,
and Dave, 19, from Sandymount,
who wants to get into marketing,
leadership hints to complement
their unique personal styles.

So much for
the real world.
Now imagine a realm
where people,
as a commonplace,
get their food
out of rubbish bins.
It's not that hard.

As the problem grows,
resources are stretched,
children are starving,
territory disputed
and there is violence.
Very widespread violence.
Very public violence.

Consider, in responding,
the political leadership
that might complement
our personal political styles.

For example, the liberal left
might build more rubbish bins.
The liberal right
might build
more secure rubbish bins.

The hard left would
control the means of production.
The hard right would
control the controllers
of the means of production.

The market liberals
might create incentives
to encourage investment
and entrepreneurial development
in the burgeoning rubbish bin sector.

The market centrists
might license rubbish bins
and rubbish bin providers
for minimum standards
of service and safety.

Pragmatic economists
would call for
the introduction of measures
to ward off the threat
of a rubbish bin bubble
in the current overheated climate.

Keynesians would wish
to increase spending
on rubbish bin services
to combat recession.

Idealistic economists
would remind us
of the immutable laws
of demand and supply.

Community leaders
might question the suitability of
particular types of bin service
in their own areas.
Community activists
would demand parity
of bin provision

with the other traditions
in our society.

Rural politicians
might complain of the danger
of under-binning
outside the urban areas
and its catastrophic effects
on the fabric of country life.

Farmers would demand and get
subsidised bins and
bin set aside schemes.

Family doctors
would seek subsidies
towards the cost
of practice bin management
for the direct benefit
of patients and wallets.

Ambitious surgeons
would attend conferences
on emerging developments
in clinical bin use
in some of the best
skiing and golf areas
in the world.
Municipal conferences
for local councilors
would stick to the golf areas.

Advocates for
the unemployed
would seek bin retraining.

Advocates for minority groups
would seek greater equality
of bin access.

Advocates for the people
eating out of the bins
would be disregarded
as merely the voices
of vested interests.

Administrators
would make the point
that they are constrained
by the paucity of existing resources.

Policy makers
would stress the need
to examine the issues closely
and to benchmark against
international experience.

Religious leaders
might decry our concentration
on the accumulation
of binly assets
at the expense of
the common and spiritual good.

Sociologists
might question
the political economy
of the issue.

Ethnologists
might discern
a thread of heritance,
a cultural legacy.

Paeleontologists
might just
keep on digging.

Poets would argue
the role of the artist
and demand to be slept with
because they are poets.

Novelists, being
nearer the money
but far from the glamour,
would keep the head down,
thinking it better
food than manuscripts.

Playwrights would workshop
starvation and struggle
and painters would simply
be in at the bins.

Although our people
would still be fighting
over food
dumped in rubbish bins,
the one thing that we,
as a diverse, resourceful,
innovative, modern and resilient society,
would proudly not lack
would be leadership.
The leadership we want.
The leadership we need.
Leadership that fits.

Crepuscular
Patrick Kehoe

Sometimes, memory of indigo night
Or sense of the place without its skin,
Young lovers in a photo finish.

Crepuscular, pastel-tinted shrouds
Cloud the walls of Barrio Gótico.
Nightwalker, I wandered here

Players of viols and sackbuts
Chasing through the Gothic alleys
Typhoid in the drains, wormwood.

Dumb waiter, approach the city
By way of Albéniz, Granados, Tarrega
The lamenting of the choirs

Excavators of the remembered city.

Danse Macabre
Annie Bell-Davies

The footprints in the wet sand stopped at a young girl, five or six, maybe. She was jumping so her bare toes and her shadow seemed to disconnect into two separate beings. The shadow lived for a tiny moment in a wavy, parallel-universe, without thought or consciousness, free from the solid, smiling reality of the girl.

Sunlight struck the curve of her bare arms and I realised then, from the uniformity of her pose, that she was practicing her ballet. I wondered what tune played in her head. As I watched, I wanted to imagine the grace of Tchaikovsky; Swan Lake or the Waltz of the Flowers perhaps. But the perfection of the image was marred by my logic. It was more likely a pensioner's fractured tinkering, on an out of tune piano that this child heard. However unfulfilling I found this thought, the girl continued to dance. She drew her lips over a gap-toothed smile. She was happily oblivious of my attention and I felt the first prickle of interest peck at my gut like a gull.

Her dress ended at her knees. I was too distant to see the detail but there was a pattern on the soft fabric, polka dots or dark hearts perhaps, against the cheerful, daffodil yellow of the cloth. Her eyes too were too distant to discover their true colour. I imagined them blue below the clipped-back, Shirley Temple mass of curls that gleamed in the sunlight like a pansy's heart.

The breeze carried a giggle to my ears, a sound so soft that it teased against the fine hair on the curve of my ear before, in cruel abandonment, it travelled on towards the rocks that jutted from the sea like un-cleaned teeth. I closed my eyes trying to hold on to the sound, to capture the happiness that lay at its heart; the feeling that I greedily sought. But I could not re-live it and I opened my eyes and felt my envy stir as I looked at her prance in front of me, taunting me, teasing me, daring me.

Out at sea, the clouds grumbled resolutely towards us, sending in the breeze that billowed and flapped her skirt above those jumping feet. The air tasted of salt but there were other flavours too, sweet and sour; sun cream and ice-cream, wet dog and human sweat. I licked my lips, dried by the air, and swallowed the taste down where it fed the waiting gull.

Then, my attention was arrested by a flash of pink. Another figure emerged from behind the girl. It was a smaller version of the yellow dancer. Maybe it was this child's laughter that had reached me. My attention moved to her and I watched. I soon realised that this was not the laughing child. The toss and turn of diamond edged waves were limp and impotent by the time they reached her. Yet this girl bent to study the thrust and tug of the tide, as it pushed and sucked the sand from between her toes with the intensity of a scientist. As the tide ebbed further out, she stepped forward to keep up with its elusive edge. Her distance from the dancer increased in jerky time.

She disappeared again as her sister, for surely these blonde angels were siblings, danced back to block my view; a pawn protecting her queen from this sly knight.

I moved. A silent, unseen side step, to avoid the bright bobbin, restored the scientist to my view. It had been a second, maybe less, but I missed her presence in my world as acutely as a desert misses rain.

I decided to name them, to make them mine. The dancer, swaying in time to an unheard melody, I named Daisy. The other, the one with the hem of her dress dipping in and out of the tide's swell, the one who held me in her spell, I named Zoe. Life!

The distance between the girls increased as Zoe chased the waves. Then she was gone. No-one else noticed. The distant bark of sandy dogs, fresh from chasing sticks in the sea and the high pitched screech of children caught in their spray continued unspoilt. Only I felt her loss. She was playing dare with the sea and it had snatched her away. Only I noticed. The shock numbed my arms, my legs, my voice.

No parents came screaming. Daisy danced on and I, deafened by my own heartbeat, slid from behind my paralysis and ran.

Daisy's gentle laughter morphed into a fretful whimper and I saw her cross her legs and dance a different jig as my long strides covered the distance between us. But she was of no interest to me now. I raced past her into the surf, ignoring the darts of ice that speared through to my veins, chilling my blood. As I continued to pound through the waves, my eyes frantic to catch a glimpse of pink beyond the grey, green silt, I felt panic rise to my throat. I had reached the spot where she vanished but there was nothing – just the endless roll of waves as they beat against my hips and their sly seduction at my ankles.

There was a commotion on the beach but I did not turn.

As I waded further into the sea my foot struck an object. It was not hard or piercing like rock, not nimble as a fish, it was soft and dull on my toes. Without further thought, I held my breath and dived beneath the surface. The pain of the cold water as it surrounded my head and attacked my brain from each facial orifice halted me briefly before my hands frantically searched for her. I needed my sight. I groped wildly at seaweed and sand and grit. I opened my eyes and shook away the burn of salt. I saw her at once; a shapeless shadow in the murky water, moving on the tide's whim. I reached out at the first piece of flesh I could grasp. I tugged at a leg and pulled her towards me and once she was safe in my arms, I kicked down on the shifting sand beneath me and pushed us back up into the air.

She hung limp and pale in my arms and I hugged her tight to my breast hoping that if I held her close enough my heartbeat would suffice for us both. I strode out of the sea with tears burning like acid as they fell from my eyes. Anonymous hands pulled Zoe from me as I came out of the surf and I felt hands on my back, thankful, congratulatory hands.

Misunderstanding.

I watched as a man with blond curls frantically pushed at her chest and forced air from his mouth to hers. I stood staring at my little scientist and willed her to live up to her name. When a gasp ended suddenly in a vomit of seawater my relief was surprising. How quickly this tot had weaved her spell on me. As her eyes opened and she fixed her blue eyes on mine and I saw the innocence and goodness that I had lost, I knew she would never be mine. Yet I was hers; completely. Above, a gull cawed as it circled us.

Finders, keepers

Maggie Breen

she jeers
as she grabs the silver key
from my hand,
dangles the key ring of the
painted, wooden girl
in my face.

Don't follow me,
she warns.

I sit on the bench
in the school shed,
knees pulled up
to my chest
and clean my nose
in the sleeve
of my brown, duffle coat.
I wait for someone
to find me,
but nobody comes.

Years later, I still mourn
the lost, wooden girl
and am convinced,
now more than ever,
that she had my eyes.

A DERELICT SITE IN AN IMAGINARY TOWN
Eamonn Wall

(1)

Rubble and dust have settled down, a clock
circles firm monotony above the town.
Local people walk street-side of the striped
hoarding to which bill-posted invitations cling.
Discharged now in walkers' eyes, the dust
bedded down by rain. All accept this site
is derelict. Next weekend, buses leave
for Knock at half-past nine. An English circus
will soon arrive. Church bells still call
Ballyveelan's faithful to Lenten prayer.

(2)

In the capital, city of diesel and feta cheese,
on a high stool over a drafting board,
an architect knows that to draw is to make
flesh. He left his village to seek in the capital
the certain curve of steel, the marble cool,
the view from the café window of the south-
bound traffic. He reveres all that promises
inaction, evasion, erasure. Rural towns
are the terra nullius on which he invents
the future. He sees rain falling on capped
heads in washed-out corners of the state.

(3)

In those washed-out corners of the state,
No child knocks on the old storyteller's door,
the piano teacher has turned her face
to the garden wall to count the climbing slugs,
no one volunteers to write our history down.
The chorus has departed another rural town.

(4)

The town manager's great brown desk
is placed to block the narrative of the poor.
He has fixed on his full-deep trousers
many charts and maps and an impressive
array of multi-coloured envelopes,
his lap a zone of cool. He bangs away
on his keyboard as old prints
of planter houses that form a backbone
of the town gather dust about his yellow
walls. There's a twiddling of thumbs,
a sigh, a call to coffee with the staff,
a pause on a downward step to ponder
a five-iron struck at dog-leg number nine
when he flirted, for one shining moment,
with the captain's prize. His assistant
lets the manager know that a developers'
queue has formed in the lane outside,
Dublin designates retail the derelict site.

(5)

From my far-suburban home, on the distant
fringes of our capital, I have made a brief
return to Ballyveelan to conduct a day
of business with a well-known merchant
of the town. On a bench in Ceannt Square,
with an hour to kill, I share an Abrakebabra
take-a-way with an old man, ragged
and wise, who is seated close beside me.

(6)

He says, in truth all towns remain contested
ground, and all of us have of late been
compromised. Every year I see my pension
rise and, for no good reason, it is raised
again. He wears a Crombie coat, top hat,
pulls hard on an old clay pipe. Be careful
not to judge too harshly, he scolds me.
Though I may look rough today, he adds,
my house, no South Fork to be sure, is at
least as well-situated as your own. I have
just returned from a week's hard-boozing
in the Gaeltacht of West Cork. Though
that derelict site across the way might seem
to you a no-man's-land, our town can not
be reckoned a Van Diemen's Land: you
should not count locals here as aborigines.
Though the manager will surely stamp

any space the architect invents—feats
they have in their compass to achieve—
they will not erase from me the day
one May I climbed three steps to the foyer
on my glorious wedding day. The derelict
site is much alive in me. For many years,
I returned there to play: my fiddle tuned,
my bow ready to strike for all the rebel
note. The capital guides not the beating
heart, he flourished as he rose. He flung
our kebab wrappers toward the middle
of the Square. Long-versed in city ways,
I sought out the elusive rural, rubbish bin.

Revolutionaries
Waylon Gary White Deer

It was 1968. There was me and Sherm and Ed in front of the girl's dorm over by the big trees when Rickey Harjo and The Stabber walk by. They want to talk to just me so I leave Sherm and Ed who are worried because their ex-girlfriends started calling them Sherman the Vermin and Sweaty Eddie. I don't like hanging around those guys much anyway in case all those girls they keep offending give me some kind of stupid nickname too.

It turns out that The Stabber wants to know if I will chip in after chow hall. He has a runner all lined up. A runner is someone over 18 who will buy us alcohol. It sure beats drinking skin bracer, which is what they call green lizard.

We go to this Indian boarding school in Santa Fe that doesn't have hardly any runners. Sherm has a fake I.D. that is no good because it says he is 53 even though he thinks it will work someday. So now I wonder who The Stabber has lined up for us after supper.

At chow hall, as usual, we are having government rations. What they call commodities. There are Navajos and kids from Alaska and Pueblos and Siouxs here. There are Oklahoma Indians and Chippewas and Yakimas and tribes I never heard of before. At chow hall tribes kind of sit by themselves but in town we all watch out for each other because sometimes people don't like Indians and they don't care what tribe you are.

So anyway after chow hall, Rickey Harjo and The Stabber and me are waiting on our runner. Rickey Harjo is from Oklahoma City but The Stabber is from some rez way up by Canada. He wears sunglasses even at night and has a long ponytail. The one thing about The Stabber is that he gets kind of political when he's buzzed. And the more he talks the more sense he makes, seems like. But this is when everybody else is buzzing too.

Well then we pay the runner and he comes back with four quarts of Garden Delite and a car. The runner is none other than Ray who is The Stabber's sort-of-brother-in-law. See last year Stabber's sister ran off from school and moved in with Ray. It's hard to tell what Ray is, at first. He says he is full blood Spanish but his mom says their dad had a lot of what they call Moro blood which is exactly why I think Ray looks like an A-rab.

All of us pile into the Raymobile and go cruising. Jimi Hendrix is on the radio. We buy big paper cups with lids and straws and we pour our wine into them. No sense getting busted right? Anyway after a while The Stabber starts talking political. What sets him off is this real tall pointy stone marker we drive by. It's right in their town square. What they call their plaza.

Nobody at our school likes the marker but we don't talk much about it. It says something like In Honor of all the Heroes killed by Savages and it's from back in the day when everybody played cowboys and Indians for real. Why they leave it up is hard to figure unless they just want to scare tourists or make Indians mad. And The Stabber is getting madder and madder but in a sort of political way.

Anyhow The Stabber starts telling us we are Indian Nationalists. Tribal governments are corrupt colonialist regimes run by business managers. Our school is a brainwashing factory. Americans are an occupying army and that big marker stands for our repression. Only when our old ways return will we be free he says. This is the real way the guy talks sometimes. Pretty soon he tells us that as Indian Nationalists it is our duty to blow up the marker. Then Rickey Harjo gets big eyes and says annit?

Like I said The Stabber starts to make sense after a while. Rickey Harjo and me are in the back seat. Stabber turns around real fast and asks us if we are in. He whips off his shades and has a drastic look like a wrestler so we both say guess so. Ray chimes in that his cousin has some dynamite stashed from when he used to work on road crew. Then Stabber's eyes light up like a pinball machine.

Ray's cousin lives in a little adobe house with a bunch of dead cars around it just like at some Indian houses. After we get there Ray grabs a flashlight and we all follow him over to this one Buick sitting up on blocks. He pops the trunk which is full of old dusty clothes. From somewhere down in the bottom Ray comes up with a dynamite stick and by now we're all buzzing pretty good.

We chip in again and this time Ray buys four quarts of peppermint vodka. Then we cruise back to the plaza and it's getting late. Stabber is bossy with Ray. He tells him don't drive fast and quit running into the curb but Reyes Tijerina is Ray's real big hero and so Ray is yelling stuff like viva la raza! At last we park in front of this high dollar tourist store with kachinas and turquoise across from the big marker. Rickey Harjo is burping really hard. I get sort of scared but I already said I am an Indian Nationalist.

Then The Stabber acts like a commando. He wraps the dynamite in his jacket and zigzags across the street except by now there's nobody else around. Then he yells Hey! Ray! Got any fuses? See we forgot to ask Ray about that earlier. All of a sudden Rickey Harjo falls out of the door and barfs up on the sidewalk. He starts rolling around too like a dog. Anyway it's right then that this cop car comes cruising around the corner of the plaza.

Instead of playing it cool Stabber zigzags away. I pick Rickey Harjo up and we take off running. Ray makes a fancy U-turn and burns rubber past a big Spanish church. Me and Rickey Harjo hide in this alley until he gets crazy and tries to fight me. So I dump him and sneak back to the school. After all that, Rickey Harjo staggers over to Ray's house and those guys all peek through the curtains with the lights off for maybe four hours.

Well the cops nab The Stabber but not before he ditches that dynamite in a dumpster. Anyway they drive him straight to his dorm after yelling at him and calling him a hippie. See those cops are Spanish and they know the Raymobile. It turns out one of them is married to Ray's sister so they give Stabber a sort-of-brother-in-law break. Go figure.

Back at school Stabber and me are sentenced to kitchen duty because we missed bed check. And they put Rickey Harjo on probation for him being gone all night. Meanwhile The Stabber tells us that dynamite is sure to go off sooner or later so we better all split up. I start hanging out with Sherman the Vermin and Sweaty Eddie again until their ex-girlfriends give me a stupid nickname too. It's one I can't say but it means that my whatchucallem is too little which isn't true by the way.

Sometimes when it is good and dark Rickey Harjo and Stabber and me go behind our dorm and drink wine with Ray. Then Stabber makes what you call a prophecy. He says someday no matter where we are, we will all feel the sound of that dynamite. When it blows up we will all feel it. That will be the sign. Then changes will come like a whirlwind faster and faster until finally our old ways will return. Listen with your hearts says The Stabber. Listen so you can feel the coming whirlwind.

All that winter we listen. We listen when we sit in class and we listen at chow hall. When we do our details we listen. We listen when we walk the girls back to their dorm. We lie on our beds and listen. We keep on listening until school lets out and we all go home.

Rickey Harjo gets drafted and they ship him off to Vietnam. Ed drops out of school and Sherm is killed in a big car wreck. The paper said he was 53. Stabber goes back to his rez and they say now he's a bad alcoholic. Ray and his old lady get fat and start having kids. I graduate from welding school. Many years pass away and I don't think about Santa Fe much anymore.

But sometimes when I lie on my bed, the wind will come whirling by my window. In my heart I can feel those days again. And so I listen.

Neurotic Girl

Westley Barnes

I'm looking for a Neurotic Girl
someone who will break down before I do
someone who's not afraid to cry,
as the tea kettle boils,
after telling me about her problems.
Someone I can worry about,
and do unselfish things for,
and offer some comfort to,
someone who depends on me for a change.
I'm looking for a girl
who isn't too confident in herself,
even though she's wonderful,
at least in my eyes.
Someone who hasn't
got her entire life sorted out, just yet.
Someone who'll realize that I can be
a nice person, behind the facade.

Because these days
I'm wandering from party to party
from pointless
city centre venues
and all-too-familiar and
contemptible small town social haunts

and all I see and hear
are the attention-seeking,
the unreachably friendly, the distant
and the involved
All swimming in mediocrity
If you'll pardon the fake sophistication
of that last metaphor
And all I'm left to do
is wonder what it would be like
to find someone
who I could be Introspective,
Debauched and Nihilistic with.
A nice Neurotic Girl.

But I suppose that would invariably lead to
some sort of responsibility
in my otherwise self-absorbed existence
I would have to pretend that I am a proper
kind of person
for the sake of my fragile lover's
 much needed feeling of security
I would take it upon myself
to go out into the world
to keep a sort of balance for the both of us
spending headache-inducing hours
with people who I can't stand
while she sits at home and smokes
in bed.

END NOTES

1) "While We Sleep," by Dermot Bolger, is taken from T*he Venice Suite: A Voyage Through Loss*, published by New Island Books.

2) "Community Matters," by Clare Scott, was written in response to a theme suggested by Coracle: Social Enterprise, Wales and Ireland. It is intended to be read aloud as part of an after-dinner speech, and adjusted accordingly to meet this medium. The poet includes Celtic associations, which would suggest the two countries and their customs.

3) The selection "Loose Haiku," by Maeve O'Sullivan, is taken from the collection, Initial Response, from Alba Publishing (2011) www.albapublishing.com

3) "Mare Rubrum," by Helena Mulkerns was originally shortlisted for the Francis MacManus Short Story Award, and broadcast on RTE Radio 1 in January, 2011.

4) "Lines Inspired By Flamenco Sketches," was written specifically to be performed at a Cáca Milis Cabaret, by two voices, to the accompaniment of "Flamenco Sketches," the last track on Miles Davis' *A Kind of Blue*, to reflect Davis' and John Coltrane's melodic warmth and sense of welcoming.

5) "Asylum" by Margaret Hawkins is extracted from her book, *Restless Spirit - The Story of Rose Quinn* published by Mercier Press (2006)

AUTHOR BIOS

ANNIE BELL-DAVIES When her primary school teacher suggested that he would be proud if any of his pupils grew up to become writers, the 8 year old Annie's hand shot into the air and her fate was sealed. Having realised her path and her purpose, she began to write stories and has been writing ever since. Her work has been published by Parthian and D.C Thomson. When not at her desk, she can be found trekking around various parts of Eastern Europe and Asia.

ANTHONY JONES was born in Carmarthen, South West Wales, where, having studied Physical Sciences at Oxford Brookes University, he has now returned to live. On a Creative Writing course there, he formed the company 'write4word' with three like-minded friends, whose mission is to promote the written and spoken word. He has led writing workshops throughout West Wales and is co-founder of "Poems and Pints at the Queens," now an essential part of the Welsh writing scene. He and his artist wife share their house with a Lurcher and five cats 'smuggled in' by his wife when she was a veterinary nurse.

BILLY ROCHE is an Irish playwright and actor. He was born and still lives in Wexford. Billy's acclaimed Wexford trilogy comprising of *A Handful of Stars* (1988), *Poor Beast in the Rain* (1989), and *Belfry* (1990) won him awards in both

Ireland and Britain. Billy's other work includes *Amphibians*, *The Cavalcaders*, the screenplay for *Trojan Eddie*, and *On Such as We*. Billy's most recent play, *Lay Me Down Softly*, received its first performance at the Peacock Theatre in Dublin in 2008. His book, *Tumbling Down* was first published in 1986. Billy's acting credits include *Aristocrats*, T*he Cavalcaders*, *Trojan Eddie*, *Man About Dog*, and *Eclipse*, an IFTA-winning film based loosely on a short film of his. In 2007, Billy was elected a member of Aosdána.

CHRIS OZZARD was born in Greyshott, Surrey in 1958. He has lived in Wales since 1979. He's a poet, writer, editor and publisher who has been sporadically published in small press limited editions. He has edited magazines such as *Kite* (1986-89), Site (1989), and *Fire* (with Jeremy Hilton, 1993-95). He now lives in Carmarthen, Wales and is part of the team that run the Oriel Myrddin Gallery. His collection of his selected poems, *Raft*, is due for publication in 2015.

CLARE SCOTT – spent her earliest years in Nigeria, West Africa and continued a restless lifestyle, gathering a wealth of experience, which included working as a teacher, social worker, sexual health professional and as a specialist in learning differences. She finally came to rest in West Wales where she has immersed herself and family of four children in the rural landscape and the culture of this region, which has a history of poetry created as the spoken word. The themes of her work are the spirit of place and human relationships, both in the natural environment, with self and with others.

DAVE LORDAN is a writer, editor and creative writing workshop leader based in Dublin. He is the recipient of the Patrick Kavanagh Award (2005), the Rupert and Eithne Strong Award (2008) and the Ireland Chair of Poetry Bursary Award (2011) for his collections *The Boy in The Ring* and *Invitation to a Sacrifice*, both published by Salmon. In 2010, his debut play, *Jo Bangles* ran at the Mill Theatre; in 2013, Wurm Press published his short fiction debut, *First Book of Frags*. He teaches contemporary poetry and critical theory on the MA in Poetry Studies at the Mater Dei Institute of DCU. See more: www.davelordanwriter.com

DERMOT BOLGER is an Irish novelist, playwright, poet and publisher, recognised as one of Ireland's most prolific and talented writers. He was born in Finglas, a suburb of Dublin, and in 1977 Bolger set up Raven Arts Press, which he ran until 1992, when he co-founded New Island Books. He has published, thus far, a dozen novels, one novella, over fifteen plays, including "The Ballymun Trilogy" and an adaptation for the stage of James Joyce's Ulysses. He has been honoured by multiple literary awards. He has also published research and non-fiction work, contributes to community literature and drama projects, and writes frequent articles for publications in Ireland. See: www.dermotbolger.com

DOMINIC WILLIAMS coordinated a series of literary initiatives for The Coracle project between 2010 and 2013, including arranging and delivering workshops, organising various events, cultural exchanges and mentorships. In 2012 he was one of three partners, the other two being national bodies Literature Wales and the National Trust, in establishing the inaugural *Dinefwr Literature Festival*. As a member of write4word, he MCs a regular monthly community-led performance event called Poems and Pints at the Queens. He has compered poetry slams in Ireland and Wales, and in 2013 curated international literary programmes for the *Pili Pala* Festival and the *Old Town Festival*. In 2013 Williams and Denis Collins set up the Wales Ireland Spoken-word and Poetry Alliance.

DRUCILLA WALL's book of poetry, *The Geese at the Gates*, is available from Salmon Poetry, who will publish her second book in 2014. Her poems, essays, and stories appear in *The Artistic Atlas of Galway*, *Free State Review*, *Cream City Review*, *Kalliope*, *Red River Review*, *Eighteenth Century Life*, and she has been anthologised in *The People Who Stayed: Southeastern Indian Writing After Removal*; *Eating Fire, Tasting Blood: Breaking the Great Silence of the American Indian Holocaust*; and *True West: Authenticity and the American West*. She holds a Ph.D. in English from the University of Nebraska and works as an Associate Teaching Professor and Poet in Residence at the University of Missouri-St. Louis.

EAMONN WALL is an Enniscorthy native who now lives in Missouri. His books include *Sailing Lake Mareotis* (Salmon Poetry, 2011) and *Writing the Irish West* (University of Notre Dame Press, 2011). He has edited two volumes of essays by the Co. Wexford poet James Liddy: *On American Literature and Diasporas* and *On Irish Literature and Identities* and these were published by Arlen House in 2013. With Paul O'Reilly and Niall Wall, Eamonn is one of the founders of Scallta Media. See: www.eamonnwall.net

EMER MARTIN is a Dubliner who has lived in Paris, London, the Middle East, and the U.S. Her first novel, *Breakfast in Babylon* won Book of the Year 1996 at Listowel Writers' Week and was published by Houghton Mifflin in the U.S. in 1997. *More Bread Or I'll Appear*, her second novel, was published internationally in 1999. Her third book, *Baby Zero*, was published March 2007. Having studied painting in New York, she has had two sell-out solo shows at the Origin Gallery in Harcourt St, Dublin. She has also worked in the medium of short film, releasing *Unaccompanied* in 2011, and producing Irvine Welsh's directorial debut NUTS in 2007. Emer was awarded the Guggenheim Fellowship in 2000, and now lives in California. See: www.emermartin.com

EOIN COLFER was born in Wexford and attained worldwide recognition in 2001, when the first *Artemis Fowl* book became a New York Times Best Seller. Having graduated from UCD and qualified as a primary school teacher, he first worked in Wexford, but later travelled with his wife, working in Saudi Arabia, Tunisia and Italy. His first book, *Benny and Omar* was published in 1998. In addition to his wildly-popular *Artemis Fowl* series, which has recently been sold for film, the author has added crime fiction to his repertoire, with his two best-sellers, *Plugged*, and *Screwed*. Eoin Colfer currently resides in Wexford,

ERIN FORNOFF is a native of the Appalachian mountains of North Carolina, an American poet living and working in Dublin, Ireland. She has extensively performed her poems live in Ireland, featuring on RTE's Arena Stage and many venues and festivals. She was a finalist at Literary Death

Match Dublin with Peter Sheridan and her essays have been published in The Irish Times. Her poetry won the StAnza Digital Slam in 2013, First Prize for Poetry in The Cellar Door, and was shortlisted for the Over the Edge New Writer of the Year for 2012 and 2013. She won Third Prize in the Strokestown International Poetry Award in 2013.

HELENA MULKERNS has written for *The New York Times, Rolling Stone, The Irish Times, Hot Press,* and *The Irish Echo,* among others. After freelancing in Paris and New York, she worked as a Press Officer for the UN in Guatemala, Africa and Afghanistan. Her short fiction has been internationally anthologised and shortlisted for the Hennessy Literary Awards, America's Pushcart Prize and the Francis MacManus Short Story Award. She holds a Masters in English Literature and Publishing from NUIG, and in 2003, she edited the anthology, *Turbulence - Corrib Voices*. She has received a bursary from the Arts Council of Ireland to complete a novel, and publishes a short story collection in 2014. See: www.helenamulkerns.com

JACKIE HAYDEN has been living in Wexford since 1996. He has published ten books, including *A Map of Love* (about the poet Dylan Thomas), and *My Boy*, the number-one bestselling story of rock star Phil Lynott, based on interviews with Lynott's mother Philomena. He has also edited four books and, as Contributing Editor to *Hot Press* penned thousands of reviews and news stories, while also interviewing a wide range of subjects, including Bob Geldof, Michael D Higgins, The Corrs, Johnny Giles and Gerry Adams. Hayden also lectures on music careers and writing.

JIM MAGUIRE's books include *Quiet People: Korean Stories* (Lapwing) and, most recently, *Music Field* (Poetry Salzburg). He is a past winner of The Strokestown International Poetry Competition.

KATE DEMPSEY's poetry and fiction is widely published in Ireland and the UK. She won the Plough Prize for a short poem and was shortlisted for the Hennessy New Irish Writing Award for both poetry and fiction. Her dinky poetry book *Some Poems* was published in 2011 by moth editions. Look for the Poetry Divas on Facebook and twitter @PoetryDivas as well as her well-read blog: www.emergingwriter.blogspot.com.

KEVIN CONNELLY lives in Duncannon, Wexford. He has read in the Wexford Arts Centre in the Cáca Milis Cabaret on Imeall, the Arts programme on TG4. He regularly reads at Harry's Bar in Kilkenny; The Fusion Cafe, Wexford; and at Hooked on Poetry, a poetry group he established in the Hook Peninsula area. His poetry has received awards in the Black Diamond Poetry Competition, the Frances Browne Poetry Competition and Fish Publications Poetry. Kevin's poems have been published in *Boyne Berries, the dVerse Anthology, The Lilliput Express* and by the Writers on Board Scheme of the Carnegie Library in Kilkenny.

MARGARET BREEN Published in *The Stinging Fly, The Scaldy Detail* and *Network Magazine*, Maggie Breen has been writing since as far back as she can remember. Her debut collection of poetry *Other Things I Didn't Tell*, published by Scallta Media in January 2013, is an exploration of self, a paring back of memories, events, addiction and depression, to reveal the truth beneath. Originally from Monageer, Co. Wexford, she now lives in Dingle, Co. Kerry.

MAEVE O'SULLIVAN lectures in media and writes poetry and haiku. Her first collection of haiku, *Initial Response*, was published in 2011. Her first regular poetry collection, *Vocal Chords*, is published in February, 2014 and her second book of haiku, *Changing the River*, in June 2014, both from Alba Press. Maeve is a founder member of Haiku Ireland and conducts workshops in haiku. For more, visit @ writefromwithin

MARGARET HAWKINS Wicklow-born journalist and health columnist with the Irish Farmers Journal, Margaret lives in County Wexford. Her first book, *Restless Spirit: The Story of Rose Quinn*, was published by Mercier Press in 2006. She has had one-act plays staged, short stories published and her radio essays have been broadcast on RTE's Sunday Miscellany and included in two of the programme's anthologies. Her debut novel, *Deny Me Not*, as well as a second edition of *Restless Spirit*, are now available. See more at: www.margarethawkins.ie

NIALL WALL's published writings include prose, poetry and music reviews. A founding member of creative writers initiative "LaunchPad", Niall is also a director of "Scallta Media" publishing group. Probably best known as a traditional singer, Niall is one of the finest exponents of the genre and is a double All-Ireland champion as a singer and songwriter. A UCD Commerce graduate, Niall is currently completing an MBA in Professional Arts Management in IT Carlow. His current projects include a novel and an album of traditional singing due for release in 2014.

ORAN RYAN is a writer living in Dublin. He has written novels: *The Death of Finn* (Seven Towers, 2006) *Ten Short Novels by Arthur Kruger* (Seven Towers, 2007), and *One Inch Punch* (Seven Towers, 2012). Plays: *Don Quixote has Been Promoted* (2009, Ranelagh Arts Festival) for the Stage and radio: *Preliminary Design For a Universe Circling Spacecraft* (KRPN, San Francisco, California, 2010). He has written and published many short stories, poetry and literary critical articles, and is currently working on his next novel, called *Hardcastle Dies Laughing*.

PATRICK CHAPMAN is the author of six poetry collections including *A Promiscuity of Spines: New & Selected Poems* (Salmon, 2012); and two books of fiction, the latest of which appears from Arlen House in 2014. He wrote the award-winning short film, *Burning the Bed* (2003), starring Gina McKee and Aidan Gillen; episodes for the childrens' TV series Garth & Bev and Wildernuts; and a Doctor Who audio play, *Fear of the Daleks*. With Dimitra ZXidous, he founded the online literary magazine, *The Pickled Body*. In 2010 his work was nominated for a Pushcart Prize. He lives in Dublin.

PATRICK KEHOE's first poems were published by the late James Liddy in broadsheets and issues of *The Gorey Detail*. Early poems were also published in the Irish Press. In recent times his work has appeared in *The Irish Times, Enniscorthy*

Echo, Natural Bridge, Cyphers and *The Scaldy Detail*. His debut collection, *Its Words You Want* was published by Salmon Poetry in July 2011. The earliest of the poems recall with striking intensity of feeling, days and nights spent in Barcelona where the poet taught English between the years 1978 and 1980.

PATRICK McCABE is a novelist, short story writer and and playwright from Co Monaghan. He has written nine novels, two of which, *The Butcher Boy* and *Breakfast on Pluto* were shortlisted for the Booker Prize for Fiction. *The Butcher Boy* also won the Irish Times Irish Literature Prize for Fiction, and both novels were adapted for film by Director Neil Jordan. He has written a children's book, *The Adventures of Shay Mouse* (1985), and a short story collection, *Mondo Desperado,* published in 1999. *Frank Pig Says Hello*, his drama adapted from *The Butcher Boy*, was launched at the Dublin Theatre Festival in 1992. His work has been broadcast on RTE and BBC, and his most recent novel is *Hello Mr. Bones/Goodbye Mr Rat* (Quercus, 2013)

PAUL HARRIS' roots are a rain-swept hill above Swansea. Following a career as a clinical psychologist and university lecturer, he is reinventing himself as a writer of prose, scripts, lyrics and poetry. He has read at the Dinefwr Literature Festival, the Carmarthen Old Town Festival, and is a regular contributor to poems and pints events in West Wales. A co-editor of the Parthian 2011 anthology, *The Month Had 32 Days*, his work has also appeared in publications like *Dawn* and the award-winning collection, *And Having Writ*. Contact him at: paulharris109@talk21.com

PAUL O'REILLY lives with his wife and children in Co. Wexford, Ireland. An award winning Irish traditional singer and musician, Paul has performed on national radio and TV. He has recorded on several albums, his fiction has been shortlisted for major awards and widely published, and he also works in both documentary and narrative film. In 2012 he was nominated for a Pushcart Prize and his film script adaptation of the Claire Keegan short story *Men and Women* won the Film Offaly Award. In 2013 the completed film was selected for the Galway Film Fleadh. See www.pauloreilly.ie

PAUL TYLAK is an Irish writer, actor and comedian. Like many Irish comedians of his generation, Paul got his first TV break on *Nighthawks*, a late night RTÉ arts, media, chat show in 1989, 1990 and 1991. Paul wrote and co-starred in two radio shows, *Hi, We're the Nualas* on RTÉ, and *The O'Show* on BBC. He is a stand-up comedian, and appears with the Dublin Comedy Improv Group. In 2003 he appeared in the play *Hurl*, written by Charlie O'Neil. His other TV credits include *Ballybraddan*, *Roy*, and *Chloe's Closet*.

PETER MURPHY is from Enniscorthy, Co. Wexford. His first novel, *John the Revelator,* was published in the UK and Ireland by Faber & Faber and in the US by Houghton Mifflin Harcourt, and nominated for the 2011 IMPAC literary award, shortlisted for the 2009 Costa Book Awards and the Kerry Group Fiction prize. His second, *Shall We Gather at the River* (2013), is published by Faber in Ireland and the UK, and as *The River and Enoch O'Reilly* in the US. He is a founder member of the spoken word/music ensemble The Revelator Orchestra, whose first album is

The Sounds of John the Revelator. Peter's journalism has been published in Rolling Stone, Huffington Post, The Irish Times, The Guardian and Hot Press magazine. He is also a reporter for RTE's arts show *The Works*.

PHILIP CASEY's novels are *The Fabulists*, *The Water Star* and *The Fisher Child*. He has published four collections of poetry, including *Dialogue in Fading Light*, and is the founder and editor of Irish Writers Online and Irish Culture. His personal online presence is at www.philipcasey.com and on twitter: @Philip_Casey.

ROSS HATTAWAY is a Dublin based poet who was born in New Zealand. Ross' first collection, *The Gentle Art of Rotting* was published by Seven Towers in 2006. Ross' work has been published all over the world and he has taken part in readings all over the world too. In 2008 he was the first Irish poet to be invited as a featured guest at the International Poetry Spring Festival in Lithuania and his work has been translated into and published in Lithuanian. He also guested at the Live Poet's Society Reading in Sydney in July 2008, and Manhattan's East Village Saturn Sessions in June 2009.

SARAH MARIA GRIFFIN is an Irish writer living in San Francisco. She graduated from NUIG with a MA in writing. Her first collection of poetry/poetic prose, *Follies*, was released by Lapwing Publishers (Belfast) in April 2011. Other poetry/prose has been included in *Oh, Francis, SouthPaw Literary Journal*, *PUSH Magazine* (UK), *Wired Ruby, Daydreamer Magazine, 3am Magazine*, Upstart Blog/Upstart

Poster Campaign, *Minus9Squared*. Other publication credits include *Raft Magazine, Boyne Berries, Pank* (US), *The Stinging Fly* and *Poetry Bus*. She is an online contributor for *The Stinging Fly* Blog, Writing.ie, and Litseen.com

SIMONE MANSELL-BROOME was born in West Wales to a Welsh father and English mother. She has taught English, EFL and Speech and Drama and worked in businesses for over twenty years - admin, PR, marketing - most hats worn at some time. She now co-runs a growing centre for courses, holidays, workshops and events (including weddings) located on an organic farm in North Carmarthenshire - www.ceridwencentre.co.uk She enjoys both page and stage, and has had three volumes of work published work so far: *Not exactly getting anywhere but… Juice of the Lemon*, and *Cardiff Bay Lunch*.

STEPHEN JAMES SMITH is a Dubliner, writer, performer, chancer, give-us-a-goer-of-that-sure, biscuit dunker, and ice-cream lover. Stephen has won the Cúirt International Literary Festival Poetry Grand Slam and numerous other awards. His ABSOLUTE Fringe play *Three Men Talking About Things They Kinda Know About* was shortlisted for the Bewley's 'Little Gem Award 2011'. In April 2011 he was invited by Culture Ireland to recite in the iconic Nuyorican Poetry Café New York. *'Arise and Go!'* his debut album with musician Enda Reilly, was selected by Hot Press as one of the best albums of 2011. In 2012 he was invited to perform his poetry in Frankfurt, Paris and in London. Find him online at: www.StephenJamesSmith.com

SUSAN LANIGAN At fifteen, Susan won a nationwide letter-writing competition on the theme, "How Can We Prevent Hunger in the World". Since graduating from NUI Galway in 2003 with a Masters in Writing (first class honours), she has published a considerable number of short stories, and has been shortlisted three times for the Hennessy New Irish Writing Award (2005, 2009, and 2012). She has also been shortlisted for the Fish Short Story Award (2011) and the Bristol Prize (2010), and longlisted for the Raymond Carver short story award in 2011 and for the Paris Literary Prize in 2013. *White Feathers* is her first novel.

SUZANNE POWER has written novels, short stories, memoir, columns and poetry. Her work has been published internationally. She also teaches creative writing at NUI Maynooth and has helped many writers to publication.

TOM MOONEY is the Group Editor of the Wexford Echo since 1996. He has won two awards for investigative journalism, The Law Society Media Award and the Amnesty International Media Award. He was the first recipient of the Mary Raftery Investigative Journalism Bursary in 2013. He published *With This or Upon This*, a book of poems, prose and photographs, with Padraig Grant, and his book, *All The Bishops Men*, was published by The Collins Press in 2011. He has edited an anthology of contemporary poetry, which will be published in November 2013, *Dust Motes Dancing in the Sunbeams*. He lives with two cats, which could be three or four by the time you read this.

WAYLON GARY WHITE DEER's memoir, *Touched by Thunder* was published in Ireland by Currach Press and in America by Left Coast Press. Recipient of a 2013 Listowel Writers Week residency, his solo painting exhibitions have shown, among other venues, at the Irish Cultural Center of New York and the American Embassy, Dublin. He has appeared in film and television productions for Turner Broadcasting, RTE, BBC, PBS, and National Geographic Explorer. He has lectured at many institutions, from Vanderbilt University to the Irish Film Institute, and while representing the 1847 Choctaw donation to Famine Ireland he was received by President Mary Robinson.

WESTLEY BARNES is originally from Wexford town. He's a recent graduate of the American Literature MA program at University College Dublin and a former auditor of UCD's English and Literary Society. At UCD he organised the financing and production of two editions of a student literary journal entitled *The Bell*. He has read his poetry at numerous literary events and is currently writing his debut novel.

Photography

We have been very lucky at Cáca Milis in that some wonderful and talented photographers have chosen to cover the event, whom we mention in the acknowledgements. Special thanks, however, to Alan Mahon, Arek Wnuk and Filip Naum for their long-standing support.

Front Cover: © Alan Mahon

Back cover, clockwise, from top left:
Peter Murphy © Alan Mahon
Kate McKenna, at Piano: © Arek Wnuk
Stephen James Smith © Alan Mahon
Emer Martin © Cold24 Photography
Ewa Barbiarczek © Arek Wnuk
Chris Ozzard © Arek Wnuk
Alex Caulfield, Helena Mulkerns © Patrick Hogan
Eoin Colfer reads from his phone © Filip Naum

Tara press